# Rocking to
# Different Drummers

*To Gigi*

*A Bright and Lovely Spirit!*

*Come journey with us through these pages . . . Enjoy!*

*My Warmest Love & Blessings,*

*Pauia (Sharon)*

# Rocking to
# Different Drummers
## Not So Identical Identical Twins

Sloan Rogers & Raina Sloan

TATE PUBLISHING
AND ENTERPRISES, LLC

Published by Tate Publishing & Enterprises, LLC
127 E. Trade Center Terrace | Mustang, Oklahoma 73064 USA
1.888.361.9473 | www.tatepublishing.com

Tate Publishing is committed to excellence in the publishing industry. The company reflects the philosophy established by the founders, based on Psalm 68:11,
*"The Lord gave the word and great was the company of those who published it."*

Book design copyright © 2014 by Tate Publishing, LLC. All rights reserved.
*Cover design by Allen Jomoc*
*Interior design by Jomar Ouano*
*Authors' photos by James Michael, Photography, Audubon, Pennsylvania*

Published in the United States of America

ISBN: 978-1-62854-091-8
1. Biography & Autobiography / Personal Memoirs
2. Family & Relationships / Siblings
14.06.04

# Dedication

As identical twin girls, you might think we had the sister we needed, kind of ready-made, no need to look any further. However, being raised with a focus on individuality, we did look beyond ourselves from early on.

We both agree that there is no one like our older sister.

Dawn, you are that sister!

Your loving spirit was like having another mom. You were enough older than us, ten years, not to want to make mud pies, but you certainly embraced us in so many special ways along life's journey, then and now.

We almost lost you recently; we would have been heartbroken.

Dawn, we are really glad that when we came along you were well on your way to creating success in your life and gratefully didn't need to compete with the inadvertent attention two look-alikes get. There might have been a touch of that, but you were a star.

You are a star!

We are blessed!

# Acknowledgments

We thank you God for the breath of life and your presence in our experience.

Dawn you have always been an amazing sister. When we came to you about writing this book, you shared our joy, and you have fostered great enthusiasm throughout the process. It has been slightly grueling at times, but you have not faltered. You have so caringly shared your unique talents, knowledge and precious time in giving much added support and suggestions throughout the formative and developing stages of our book, all of which have been welcomed and appreciated beyond measure. You have not only contributed your perceptions by adding a chapter to our text, but you have been there to shed light on facts that were a little sketchy… perhaps the ten years between us had a purpose after all. We are thankful.

Susan, Stephen, Dawn, Richard, and Cheryl, when we asked each of you if you would be willing to write a message for our book about how it felt to be a child of an identical twin, we got a resounding response saying that you didn't really identify with that question—that in the inner circle of our family it was never talked about as such. However, you did see similarities and differences that you have graciously and beautifully expressed. We find the narrations of the likenesses and differences you each experienced refreshing and enlightening, since it is something about which we rarely talked. We are grateful for your contributions and insights. You are truly wonderful and amazing children and we are so grateful to be your mothers.

We want to express our heartfelt thanks to all of our family and friends who have encouraged us to write this book. You have listened, shared thoughts, and embraced our ideas all along the way. Your understanding of the time that it would take for this treasured effort when we have given so much more of ourselves to you naturally has touched us deeply. We can now come back to that place to offer our cherished relationships more once again.

We so much appreciate those who contributed to our "How You See Me and Me" chapter. Five people shared the one word they felt best described us, Elaine or Carole. This fun little project reflects the similarities and differences in how we are viewed by those outside of our family, as well as our one sibling. To Dr. Lawrence Borow, Rev. Sheila Pierce, John Toebe, Lucy Arnold and Dawn Ganss, we say, your contributions have added a unique dimension to our book, of which you are now a part.

We are most grateful for the time effort and skills extended to us by a friend, Winfield Swanson, in reviewing our book. It was an appreciated contribution.

Our deep appreciation is also extended to Reverend Ian Taylor who graciously took time from his busy schedule to read and comment on our book. His heartfelt words are sincerely valued.

Our good fortune extends also to have the opportunity to work with Tate Publishing. They are caring and professional all the way. We know that the combined skills they bring to the table from copy and conceptual editing, to layout, to design, and to publishing will provide us with a polished book of which we will be proud.

Our project managers—Allyson Winters, Lindsey Marcus, Kate Reynolds, Fallon Casteel, and Kate Silorio—and editors, Amanda Bumgarner and Kyle Crawford, have been crucial in the formative stages. There are many facets to publishing a book and

Rachael Sweeden, Traci Nix, Cheryl Moore, and Katya Tysdale have played an important role as well. For those whose names we are not aware, but have contributed to a quality finished product we appreciate you as well.

To Stacy Baker, we want you to know how much we appreciate your foresight and vote of confidence to accept our manuscript into the Tate world of publishing.

# In Memory of Mom and Dad

Mom and Dad, this is about you and the twins you created. If not for you, there would be no story to tell.

We both unequivocally feel that the greatest gift you gave us was supporting our individual spirits. Somehow, you knew that no matter how cute or catchy it is to see twins looking exactly alike right down to their shoes, you wanted more than that for us. You wanted each of us to discover who we are and move forward accordingly... in some families, that does not happen even if you are not a twin.

Mom, in our early years you were our stronghold. You were the support that kept us alive and well for that formative period of our lives when dad was busy traveling. We clearly were a matriarchal family, the four Sloan women. Your journey was not easy and when life threw you a curve, we felt your pain. But, you persevered and eventually were able to resolve the disappointment endured. Your life revealed how to survive through the good and the bad times with grace. For seventy years, we traveled the hills and valleys together and for seventy years, we loved you.

Dad, we wish we had known you better. You were gone so much of the time, traveling to make a living for your family. It wasn't until we were in our teens that you became active in our lives. Before then, you were in and out of our lives as your work dictated, with a gift here and there... teddy bears, chuckles, and the famous bikini undies that your secretary sent us without considering our tender age. We liked them anyway. We will never forget the many moments and your special talents shared with us when you were at home. We sensed your love for us and we loved you, too.

# About Mom

Frances Thelma Dean Sloan

Life Span ~ December 13, 1912–June 21, 2011
Born and raised in Philadelphia, Pennsylvania

Wife, Mother, Sister, Aunt, Grandmother, Great-grandmother

Homemaker, Bridge Director, Bridge Instructor

Youngest of 4 sisters and 1 brother

Mother (Lily Gertrude) ~ homemaker
(McCormick Steamship Family)

Father (Ernest) ~ owned plumbing & heating business with his son
Migrated from England with his family when he was twelve

Traits/Characteristics
> Caring
> Education advocate
> Indecisive
> Intuitive
> Proud
> Reserved
> Sense of humor
> Strong sense of family
> Thrifty
> Timid

Interests included bridge, still-life painting, rug hooking, and reading

# About Dad

Stephen Alfred Sloan

Life Span: May 3, 1910—March 22, 1981
Born and raised in Vineland, New Jersey

Husband, Father, Brother, Uncle, Grandfather, Great-grandfather

Served in the US Navy, Butcher, Combustion Engineer, Inventor, Engraver

4 sisters, no brothers

Mother (Louisa)—a homemaker

Father (Stephen)—Chief Engineer at the Vineland, New Jersey Training School

Attended Drexel University

Worked at the Philadelphia Navy Yard

Retired From Peabody Engineering, Stamford, Connecticut

Invented the Sloan Igniter for Peabody Engineering, now Sun Oil Company

Engraving business for retirement years

Traits/Characteristics
    Caring
    Creative
    Dedicated worker
    Dependable provider
    Ethical
    Highly organized
    Inventive mind
    Perfectionist
    Reserved
    Unassuming

Interests included technical drawings and writing poetry, which we didn't know until finding a log after his death; (Robert Louis Stevenson—first cousin once removed). He also enjoyed engraving, and solving engineering problems.

# About Our Sister

Dawn Sloan Ganss

Life Span: August 28, 1931 –
Born in Philadelphia, Pennsylvania: Raised
in Pennsylvania and New Jersey

Sister, Daughter, Wife, Mother, Aunt, Grandmother

English Teacher, School Librarian and Coordinator, Bridge
Instructor, Homemaker

Mother: Frances Thelma Dean Sloan

Father: Stephen Alfred Sloan

Sisters: the not so identical identical twins.

Graduated from Douglass College, Rutgers University
BA: Bachelor of Arts in English Dramatic Arts, Douglass College
MLS: Masters of Library Information Science, Rutgers Graduate
School

Sixth Year Certification and credits from Rutgers Graduate
School of Library Information Science-specialties; Information
Needs and School Media Centers

Teaching Certificate in English and Social Studies, Grades 7-12
New Jersey, Department of Education certificates for: School
Librarian, Education Media Specialist and Supervisor
Certification

Participating Member of the Middle States Association of
Colleges and Schools evaluated: Hawthorne High, River Dell
Senior High, and Red Bank Catholic High Schools

Active Participation on state, regional, county, and local levels of
establishing New Jersey's Multi-type Library Network (presented
and chaired workshops; coordinated Regions III and IV-assisted
in writing *Guidelines for School Library-Media Centers*)

Children:   one son: Arthur Douglass Ganss
            one daughter: Daryl Beth Ganss

Grandchildren:   one granddaughter, Katelyn Marie Cannon
                 one grandson, Brian Thomas Cannon

Retired from Westfield High School, New Jersey; moved to and lived at the Eastern Shore in Maryland, and is currently residing at Beaumont Retirement Community in Bryn Mawr, Pennsylvania, with husband, Arthur Edward Ganss

Traits/Characteristics
  Encouraging
  Giving
  Intelligent
  Intuitive
  Lives life to the fullest
  Loving
  Modest
  Non-judgmental
  Strong sense of family
  Supportive


Interests: sports reporting, theater, reading, needlework, entertaining, writing a column, "Web Cites" for the publication *School Librarians Workshop* on best websites for K-12 students, teachers, and administrators, volunteering at the church and community center

# Contents

# Introduction

There are mega studies and articles written on twins, triplets, and multiple births all lending much speculation and enlightenment to this wonderful phenomenon, but what better way to experience some of that information than from ones who are living it.

We will be sharing some happenings and special data that speak to our likenesses but, most importantly, our differences. These facets will be addressed in a variety of formats.

First, we will share some contrasts that one may be curious about.

Often twins are asked a variety of questions as others try to discern what it must be like to have a sibling who is just like you. We have answered some of those questions for you.

In our quest for individuality, you will also see a level of independence on our parts when we tell you how each of us came to make complete name changes many years ago.

An area of particular interest when it comes to research and curiosity is within the medical arena, so we have shared some facts from this area.

As we have looked back over the years, we have been keenly aware of happenings that one might refer to as twin phenomenon and twin things. We have shared some of those with you as well.

As you might imagine, twins have their own little world of escapades, as we call them—the kind of happenings that one might refer to by saying, "What one doesn't think of, the other will."

All of these subjects are explained and discussed by one of us or as a joint perspective.

In addition, we wanted you to experience the differences and/ or likenesses as you may perceive by our having taken various happenings as well as segments of time and written about them from our own perspectives, giving you a comparative to view. These chapters were written without our discussing any of our remembrances, not knowing what the other would be writing. You will not only see compared views, but unique styles.

Included is a comparative on three personality and interest inventories we both have taken. We were surprised by the outcome and wonder if you will be also.

As you read, you will see that we have mostly referred to ourselves with our given names, Elaine and Carole.

*Elaine is Sloan*
*Carole is Raina*

# Prologue

In 1941, one didn't have the means of knowing the exact count or gender of baby "X." In the 1960s, when our children were born, we were privy to a little ritual that was purported to reveal the gender of baby-to-be.

This little ritual took place with the expectant mother lying on her back and someone holding a string with the mother-to-be's wedding band dangling from the end over her baby bump. If the ring went around in a circle it was a girl and if the ring went back and forth, a boy. We thought that was so clever, but didn't give it a lot of credence. However, it gave way to great expectations and lots of contemplation.

What we did come to observe in that process was the power of concentration. If we focused intently enough on the ring going in a particular direction, we could actually create our preference if we had one. The old wives tale concept was at play.

Twins are usually born a month early and we were no exception.

It was a cool windy day in March, budding tulip and daffodil fragrances wafting in the breeze, when our mother left for the hospital to deliver her twins. She was looking forward to her new babies and being able to "look down and see her feet once again" so it was told.

That highly anticipated, anxiety-laden drive to the hospital was interrupted when an unkempt, unfriendly stranger hopped into the back seat of our parents' car while stopped at a red light.

Mom's condition prevailed as this stranger got in one door and quickly moved across the car getting out of the opposite door. It would have seemed that the condition of the moment was not one to become a part of, especially for one displaying such deviant behavior. Helping to bring twins into this world was not on his list of priorities.

The happening was told with little drama, just as if it were one of those things that happened often and without major consequence.

It was the first day of spring, and we were about to arrive. Mom knew she was going to have twins, the doctor had reported two heartbeats. However, there was a caveat.

As to our birth, we could say, "And then there were three"... well almost. We would have had a brother, but he did not make it through the development and birthing process. The doctor informed our mother that we two were definitely from one egg thus identical twins. The fact that we might have had a brother journey along with us through life did not negate our being identical. Nor was it a fact that our mother had any knowledge of until delivery.

So, we were not only identical twins but also what is known as super twins. One version of super twins is that of the fertilization of two eggs: one being identical twins and the other in our case a male counterpart.

A side note, super twins refers to any multiple births of three or more.

A second side note, the offspring of identical twins are considered half-brothers and sisters. Our families just grew!

Fraternal twins are hereditary and represent two thirds of twin births. There are two girls or boys from different eggs or a boy and a girl from different eggs.

As to the one third of twins, who are identical, there does not appear to be any hereditary influence or known environmental contribution. It has been said that identical twins are a "freak of nature."

What is important is we shared the same space from inception. Now we are sharing the world.

This thought brings about the most important factor in our development, the *gift of individuality*. My parents gave us direction and encouragement to discover ourselves. Without individuality and the sense of autonomy that comes with it, there would be limited self-esteem. How wonderful they sensed its importance.

Individuality: what constitutes individuality? Are you familiar with the expression "dare to be different"? Well, that succinctly speaks to individuality.

What did that gift of individuality look like for us?

Summed up, we were infrequently dressed alike. There would at least be a color variance. Our mother, consciously promoting fairness, would always see that we both received the same, but the style and colors varied.

We were allowed and encouraged to have our own chosen friends and spend time with those friends without the other being included. Occasionally, if one of us was going to a special event, our mother would comment that it would be nice if the other could go.

From fourth grade on, upon moving from New Jersey to Connecticut, we were assigned to separate classrooms at school. We adjusted so quickly that it would be hard to determine the actual merit, if any. It did not impact our grades or the development of our own relationships.

Many years of our adult lives have been spent in different parts of the country and many within the same community. In either case, it did not have a major impact on our life's happenings. When not living in the same part of the country, certainly the phone was important. One does not need to be a twin for that to be the case.

In our attempt to give you a taste of an identical twin experience, you will read about:

Contrasts, personal data, life choices, name changes, medical differences and likenesses, twin phenomenon and things, pictures, escapades, comparative chapters on shared and non-shared events, comments from our children, and personality inventories.

You will notice that we definitely lean toward the side that environment plays a strong and significant role, perhaps because that gives a greater opportunity to create individuality than to feel that we had no choice.

Today, there is updated research on which to rest our thoughts. According to the *American Journal of Human Genetics*, even though identical twins share very similar genes, the twins are not identical. Imagine that.

When we hear that, a part of us wants to say, oh, but we are identical. Does the grass look greener on the other side?

Also in the March 2008 issue, research found changes in the DNA sequence between identical twins, reflected when a gene exists in multiple copies. The research did not confirm whether these changes occur during fetal development or as twins age. The research is significant, because many medical conditions can be influenced by copy number variations, such as autism, AIDS, and lupus.

For some time, there has been substantiation that identical twins will exhibit differences based on happenings within their environment. However, a new dimension has been added to the equation: epigenetics. Epigenetics are chemical markers that attach to the genes and impact how they are expressed. It can affect the particular gene by either stopping or increasing its output.

When you think about a gene expression being either stopped or increased, you can imagine the dynamics of the impact upon one.

These epigenetic changes can occur over a lifetime from smoking, diet, and even stress, *and* they have been suggested to play a part in cancer and behavioral characteristics such as fear, confidence, and the whole gamut of emotions.

These epigenetic markers vary considerably, but with identical twins, these epigenetic factors are more alike and seem to influence only the expression of the gene and not the underlying makeup.

The very first environmental effect that we are aware of occurred at birth. It didn't even require waiting to see what difference the environment had in store for us.

One of us was a natural birth, the other a forceps delivery resulting in a difference in the shape of our faces across the cheekbone area. Many have noticed and commented on this slight difference from time to time.

In *Breaking the Habit of Being Yourself,* author, Dr. Joe Dispenza states:

> Just by changing our thoughts, feelings, emotional reactions, and behaviors, for example, making healthier lifestyle choices with regard to nutrition and stress level, we send our cells new signals, and they express new proteins without changing the genetic blueprint. So while the DNA codes stay the same once a cell is activated in a new way by new information, the cell can create thousands of variations of the same gene.

A parting note, as we are planning and writing, we find something interesting. We tend to be focused on the differences and not the likenesses.

In the process of taking you, the reader, on our journey, we are prepared to learn new things about each other. We like that thought.

Happy reading!

# Contrasts and Questions

Me and You, You and Me
Together in the year 1941 we ushered in spring

CONTRASTS

|  | Elaine (Sloan) | Carole (Raina) |
|---|---|---|
| **Family Nick Names** | Lambie Pie Lanie | Cupcake |
| **Twin to Twin Nick Names** | Sloan Girl | Rayshine |
| **Birth Date** | 3/20/41 | 3/20/41 |
| **Birth Time** | 5:00 pm | 4:50 pm |
| **Length @ Birth** | 18 ½" | 18" |
| **Pounds @ Birth** | 4lbs 3oz | 4lbs 2oz |
| **Birth Process** | Forceps | Natural |
| **Height Now** | 5'7" | 5'7" |
| **Weight Now** | 137 | 137 |
| **No. children given birth to** | 2 | 3 |
| **Gender** | boys<br>Stephen (50)<br>Richard (47) | girls<br>Susan (53)<br>Dawn (48)<br>Cher (43) |

| | | |
|---|---|---|
| **Education** | AA in Psychology<br>Essex College<br>Sales & Marketing<br>Decorating Courses<br>Writing Courses | Business courses/<br>Fairfield University<br>Ministry School<br>Reiki Master |
| **Present Work Status** | Retired<br>Post Grad Program/<br>Washington School of<br>Psychiatry<br>Author | Sales & Marketing<br>Interfaith Minister<br>Reiki Master<br>Author |
| **Religious Practice** | Christian | One God<br>Christ-Conscious Life |
| **Life's Greatest Moment** | Birth of my sons | Arrival of<br>my daughters |
| **Most Important Attribute** | Honesty | Love |
| **Most Special Achievement** | Nationally Published Book | First Book in Print/<br>Graduation from<br>Ministry School |
| **Car We Drive** | Volvo Sedan | Camry XLE |
| **Hobbies** | Photography | Enhancing life's journey |
| **FAVORITES** | | |
| **Color** | Plum/Peach | Plum/Orange/Yellow |
| **Clothing Style** | Eclectic/ Stylish | Trendy/ Stylish |
| **Jewels** | Aquamarine/Pearls<br>Chocolate Diamonds | Amethyst/Diamonds<br>Pearls |
| **Decorating Style** | Traditional/<br>dark woods<br>Orientals/Art | Traditional/<br>Contemporary |

| | | |
|---|---|---|
| **Book** | *Gifted Hands*<br>By Ben Carson, MD | *Autobiography of a Yogi*<br>By Paramahansa<br>Yoganada |
| | *Whoever Said<br>Life is Fair*<br>By Sarakay Cohen<br>Smullens | *The Prophet*<br>By Kahil Gibran |
| **Poem** | "Village Blacksmith"<br>By Longfellow | "Love Poems"<br>By Rumi |
| **Music** | Jazz/ R&B/ Gospel | Smooth Jazz |
| **Movie** | "Chariots of Fire"<br>"Magnificent<br>Obsession" | "A Walk in the<br>"Clouds" |
| **Broadway Show** | "Cats"<br>"Black & Blue" | "Smokey Joe's Café" |
| **Food** | Pizza with Arugula<br>Frozen Yogurt with<br>Peanut Butter<br>Fuji apples | Peanut Butter<br>on apples/<br>Coconut Milk Ice<br>Cream |
| **Holiday** | Christmas/Birthdays | Christmas/Valentine's<br>Day |
| **Sports** | Swimming/Dancing/<br>Skating | Swimming/Dancing<br>Skating |
| **Vacation Spot** | Jamaica/Nassau/<br>Long Branch | Sedona/Miami Beach/<br>Long Branch |
| **Song** | "The Prayer"<br>and<br>"If I Could" | "I Believe"<br>and<br>"I Come to the Garden" |

# Questions Some People Ask Twins

*Do you get annoyed when called by the other twin's name?*

Elaine: Not in the slightest. Only when called "twinie" and that was years ago. Actually, my parents called me by Carole's name more frequently than those outside of the family.

Carole: No, that doesn't bother me at all.

*Do you have any special connections with your twin?*

Elaine: All my connections in life are special in their own way. This may evoke the question of whether I know her better than any other. Yes, I think so, but not in a way that is extremely unique. I was once told by a therapist that Carole and I were as close to being like any sibling relationship as twins could be.

Carole: I believe so, but I don't think it's because she is a twin. I think it is because I like who she is—a very special person and my friend.

*Do you ever wish you were a single child?*

Elaine: There is no hindrance in being a twin, so I would have to say no. I have only given thought to not being a twin when others don't recognize my individuality which happened mostly when I was young, or on occasion when one would attribute an action to "one of the twins" as if ownership of the action didn't matter.

Carole: No, I never gave that any thought. I felt blessed to have sisters, especially my sisters.

*What traits do you share?*

Elaine: Giving, intuitive
Voice intonation, the characteristic that confuses others the most

Carole: Giving, intuitive
Voice intonation, the characteristic that confuses others the most

*What are the advantages/disadvantages of being a twin?*

Elaine & Carole: We concur
Advantage: Having a companion at special times
Disadvantage: When others don't see us as individuals

*What are three ways that others can easily tell you apart?*

|  | Elaine | Carole |
|---|---|---|
| Color of our hair | Steel Gray | Blonde |
| Style of dress | Stylish | Trendy |
| Personality Style | Reserved | Outgoing |

A quick story! A number of years ago, when working in a corporate setting, Carole came in to see if I wanted to have lunch with her. I did not know she was coming by. I had already gone out. It was nearing the time I would be coming back when Carole arrived. My co-workers thought that Carole was me and that I had my hair colored on my lunch hour.

*What is the number one main difference between you both?*

Elaine: Spiritual Philosophies
   Christian based

Carole: Spiritual Philosophies
   One God

*Do your friends ever get you mixed up?*

Elaine: Over the years, many have mixed us up—parents, husbands, children and friends.

> On one occasion my godchild, three years old, saw Carole shopping in the grocery store where she was with her mother who was also shopping and kept calling "Aunt Sloan, Aunt Sloan," and got no response. She cried all the way home and then some. Her mother called my husband and asked what was wrong with Sloan. "Is everything okay?" And everything was okay. I anxiously called my godchild and tried to console her broken heart.
>
> Another day, I walked into the dry cleaners I had been using for years, and I was greeted with these words, "You won't believe it, but when your sister came into the shop yesterday, I thought it was you." I didn't have the heart to tell her it was me.
>
> My message to Carole was, if you hear my name, when you are out and about, *smile* and I will do the same. Or if one looks at you with a knowing eye, *smile* again.

Carole: When I am out and around town, Elaine's friends will see me and take a second look to be sure, and I say, "You think I am Sloan, don't you?" And they respond, "Oh you are her sister."

*Are you interested in the same activities?*

Elaine: Perhaps in part. Right now, I am loving school and am in the midst of developing workshops for the care-giving community. My constant activities include enjoying time with family, reading, writing, walking, going to museums, movies, theater, and dining out. I thoroughly enjoy art and photography.

Carole: I do not believe we have similar interests except for writing and reading. I enjoy meditating, spending time by the ocean, pursuing my passion for Reiki, and developing my company, Divine Reflections. Presenting seminars on being one's authentic self and EFT (Emotional Freedom Technique) are on my horizon.

# Name Changes

Names, names
What's in a name?
Elaine by any other name
Is still Elaine

## ELAINE BY ANY OTHER NAME IS STILL ELAINE

Elaine by any other name is still Elaine!

Why does one choose the name they do? I have come to see names as a very important tag we are given with which to live our lives… a tag that can bring us joy or on the other end of the spectrum actually cause us grief.

In my case, my parents named me Elaine and my twin sister, Carole.

Many times, people attempt to give twins "twinie" type names. However, with my mother's determination to keep us as individual as possible, that didn't happen. It did cross her mind; of course it would. Striving to keep us as individual as possible prevailed.

Elaine Marie Sloan was my given name. Two nicknames evolved from this given name: Lanie by my mom and Lambie Pie by my dad.

What motivated my mother to select the names she did? We've been told stories, Carole, with an "e" was due to my mom's attraction to the movie star Carole Lombard. The first-born, received the name Carole, but what to name baby two.

My mother's favorite aunt, Aunt Marie, was my father's aunt who she had the good fortune of sharing by virtue of marriage. Mother wanted to name me after Aunt Marie, but was reluctant because this aunt was well off and she did not want it thought that she had other motivations. There had been some comments from others in the family earlier on. So Marie became my middle name, preceded by Elaine.

Why Elaine? Perhaps she had an affinity for Camelot and, as legend would have it, named me after Lancelot's mother, or his lover of brief encounter with whom he fathered Sir Galahad, *or* I heard that mom loved the song "Maria Elena" that states, "You are the answer to my prayer." Perhaps I was.

One thing I do know is the name Elaine reached a peak of popularity in the year I was born, 1941, with 5,376 baby girls being tagged with that name.

Carole, in case you are slightly curious how many baby girls were named Carole, with an "e"—4,966.

I kept the name Elaine for forty years, at which point in my journey I decided to rename myself. I was never really attracted to my name. Actually, I would say I had indifference toward it.

My father had four sisters, no brothers, and no sons. He was the last of the Sloans. So from a sentimental aspect and a practical purpose (thinking it would be better remembered in the business arena), I changed my name to Sloan.

Years before, I missed the opportunity to name either of my sons Sloan. This was my last chance to keep the name alive a little longer.

My dear mother was accepting of my strong desire to change my name by graciously introducing me to new acquaintances in her life as "Sloan." However, I can still hear her say, "You will always be Elaine to me." And that was fine.

Some of my friends who had always known me as Elaine made a wonderful attempt to call me Sloan. If we got into a particularly serious conversation, they would revert to Elaine... kind of like a warm fuzzy blanket. So, in a rare instance, Sloan and Raina become Elaine and Carole once again.

Elaine is a form of Helen, the French version, and means, bright light.

I hope I have been a "bright light" in someone's life.

---※---

## CAROLE TO SHELBY TO RAINA

What's in a name one might ask? Would you be surprised if I told you there is energy in a name? After some research and study, I found this to be true. I also believe it becomes a part of your very essence.

When my parents realized they had two baby girls to name, my mother said to my father, "You name one and I will name the other." She had a real passion for the actress Carole Lombard and said she would name hers Carole Ann, that is me, and my father named his Elaine Marie that's my twin. Now I never heard where the Elaine came from, but I believe the Marie came from his Aunt Marie of whom she was very fond. Daddy nicknamed Elaine "Lambie Pie" and me "Cupcake." I never felt warm about that name, but he did.

Years later, Mom told me of other names that they had considered, and I was grateful they did not choose them. Some sets of names were Bethel and Rachael, Yvonne and Yvette, Lynn and Lynda. As the first-born, I would have been Bethel in that set of names, and I do believe I would have found a way to change my name long before I could speak it. It is an okay name, but not one I would have chosen for myself.

While my parents gave us the gift of true individuality, those around us did not follow suit. Because we were so much alike, we were often called "Twinie," eliminating the need for one to figure out which one of us they were communicating with, at least initially. And I do believe that, for some reason, when I was born, there must have been a run on the name Carole. Did you ever hear the saying: "When you speak of Hazel, which Hazel do you mean?" Well that is how I felt. I wanted a name different from others... one to be uniquely mine. As I am writing, something inside of me is saying, of course you did. Individuality was always emphasized.

At about forty years of age, I playfully said to Elaine, "I want a new name." She happily contributed to my whimsical moment, saying, "You remind me of a Shelby. I remember this sister of a friend of mine named Shelby and she was sweet and kind like you... and you would make a good Shelby."

I instantly agreed and started to refer to myself by my new name. It was feeling natural and for the most part, all of my friends and family had no problem with my name change and all went rather flawlessly. I soon came to find that Ford made a car known as the *Shelby*, and this was also a somewhat common man's name, but for the moment I was good. I settled into my new name for almost twelve years. Thank you, Elaine.

One day, while at work, I went to tell a customer my name, and Shelby just wouldn't come out of my mouth. Sitting and reflecting on what was happening, I realized it was time for a change... Shelby no longer.

That evening, I contemplated on what my new name would be and started to think of Reiki, a healing art that I dearly love and wanted to be a master of one day. As I was reading one of my favorite books, Reiki Healing Yourself and Others, by Marsha

Burack, I came upon the meaning of Reiki. I found that the first ideograph Rei is composed of three parts. *"The first means rain, which comes from heaven and gives life to our planet. The second represents mouth/breath or prayer; with our breath and mouth we give voice to our deepest desires and truth. The third signifies the king or master within each of us. Blessings from heaven of a kingly nature rain down upon us responding to our word."* This deeply touched my soul. This meaning coupled with "ah" the sound of creation gave birth to the name Raina. I was not sure whether to spell it Reina or Raina, but since I loved the rain and the spelling looked so pretty to me, I decided quickly on Raina. I embraced this name with such passion, and I sensed innately that while I did not start my life out as Raina I would be called Raina always.

I am now known as C. Raina Sloan. I keep the C. in honor of my mother's choice. She loved Raina and called me that from the day I made the change. It was a beautiful thing. On a rare occasion, she would say Carole, and just before she died she did ask "Where is my Carole?"

# Medical Differences and Likenesses

---

## ELAINE'S MEDICAL FACTS

When it comes to the medical realm, I kind of see Carole's and my relationship as checks and balances. As different as we see ourselves being, we still check with the other in a comparative mode when something goes wrong, health wise.

I am very much a naturalist, believing in preventative measures as opposed to running for the medical modality. Having a serious list of allergies to medications, it seems prudent to look for the natural cure above all else.

Some very wonderful medical doctors who I trust take care of needs that are not self-treatable.

With that in mind, I give attention to preventative measures and work at making healthy choices to promote optimum well-being. There are certainly times that this has not worked, but the attempt was clear.

For example, when diagnosed with Hashimoto's (a hypothyroid condition), I went immediately to a naturalist to try and circumvent the need for Synthroid or Synthroid-type medication. My internist was fine with that as long as I had regular blood tests to monitor my success or lack thereof. My naturalistic approach was not successful; therefore, the need to take Synthroid won out. However, possibilities are always an option.

Carole's and my only in-hospital surgery was a tonsillectomy… we were in about the third grade. That was an event! Neither one of us wanted to go first. Who would? Who did? Neither of us was prepared to be a trailblazer. Alas, I blazed the trail.

- Blood: Type B+
- Mitral Valve Prolapse—discovered when I passed out with a high fever in my highchair (1942)
- Third degree burns—Accident (1953)
- Fibromyalgia—Diagnosis without major impact—never treated for it (1969)
- Hematoma on the head—Serious accidental fall (1986)
- Hashimoto/Thyroid (1990s) Father had Hashimoto that was not discovered until autopsy was performed
- Herniated discs (1990s)
- Major subarachnoid bleed—healed without surgery (1994)
  Thought to have come from the fall eight years earlier
  I fell into the one percent of the population where they could not determine the cause
- Scoliosis and stenosis—first diagnosed early 2000s
- Blood clotting factor—Prothrombin II gene mutation (2012)

Labors

First son: Stephen, 10 lbs ½ oz, 23 inches long
Ten-month pregnancy, with toxemia, paralyzed bladder
and thrombosis in both arms
Fifteen-hour labor, (in incubator for three days)

Second son: Richard, barely 7 lbs, 21 inches long
Three days late
Two-hour labor, all was well

# About My Children

## ELAINE'S SONS

I am blessed to have two very caring and enterprising sons and daughters-in-law:

Stephen is fifty years old, married to a charming, successful young lady, Kim. Stephen has a degree in Accounting and his Masters in Divinity. He incorporates his accounting skills and passion for people serving as Financial Director for the city of Phoenixville, Pennsylvania.

Interests: Helps local non-profit organizations that focus on reaching out to those in need of basic assistance and a safe place to live.

Stephen often spends one week a year helping to build churches around the country.

Kim has a degree in History and Political Science and a Masters in Religious Education. She spent a number of years in the ministry, including mission work in Scotland and Paris. Now she works as an Analyst for a sales management company in Wayne, Pennsylvania

Interests: Playing guitar and photography

They share life together enjoying travel around the world, serving God in local church and community efforts, and spending time with family and friends while living in the Greater Philadelphia area.

Richard is forty-seven years old, married to a lovely, enterprising young lady, Joan. He has his Bachelor's of Science in Technology and Management and has retired from the US Army as a Major. He now uses his unique logic skills in working as Logistics Management Specialist for The Department of Defense and working on his master's degree.

Interests: Coaching baseball and 4-H Dog Shows

Joan majored in Business and has utilized her special creative talents in working with the Marriott in the Photographic Department and in managing a department within Safeway.

Interests: Scrapbooking / greeting card design

They enjoy life, taking family vacations and planning for quiet time together. They reside in western Maryland with their sons, my extraordinary and delightful grandsons, Derek, 19, and Brandon, 13.

Derek is a freshman at Mary Washington in Virginia and is a catcher on their baseball team while studying pre-med.

Interests: Baseball and trips to the ocean.

Brandon is in the eighth grade and very busy with his pets and 4-H shows with his labradoodle, Cosmo.

Interests: 4-H Dog Shows and Industrial/Commercial Equipment

Stephen and Kim

Brandon, Richard, Joan, Derek

# CAROLE'S MEDICAL FACTS

What is wellness/wholeness? Now, to most, the response is pretty natural and most likely something like feeling great and enjoying your life. My response would be, I have never truly felt a strong sense of wellness that I can remember. *What does it feel like*, I ask myself?

Of this, I am certain. My twin and I came into this world whole and healthy with no apparent maladies. Where and how did that disappear from the radar? I am not clear, but I do know it happened!

- Blood Type B+
- Birthmark on side
- Hematoma on my head treated with radiation during first year of life
- Mitral Valve Prolapse
- Mononucleosis (1967)
- Multiple Sclerosis
- Mercury toxicity (2002)
- Mold toxicity (2004)
- Cyst on half of the spleen (2004)
- Hashimoto's/Thyroid (2006)
- Blood clotting factor—Protrombin II gene mutation (2012)
- Scoliosis & stenosis
- Six herniated discs

Labors

First daughter: Susan—7lbs 6oz, 19 ½ inches long
    Arrived on her due date: 4 hours labor

Second Daughter: Dawn—7lbs 1 oz, 18 inches long
    Arrived two days early: 2 ½ hours labor

Third Daughter: Cheryl—7lbs 5oz, 18 ½ inches long
    Arrived two days late: 3 ½ hours labor

While Elaine and I do not have many of the same health issues, we seem to be a comfort to each other at those times when we want to discuss what we are feeling. Frequently, the conversation will start with, "Have you ever felt…?"

I wish I knew years ago what I know today. Yet, it is never too late. I know the body has cell memory and understanding how it works can play a significant role in your physical well-being. I believe there is a mental equivalent for every physical condition, and this is important, too. While these truths are simplistic in some regards, they are enormous in others. I know that this knowledge along with a few other lifestyle choices has played a major role in the MS diagnosis of twenty-eight years not progressing. I never embraced the diagnosis on any level and always proclaimed it would never have its way with me. Then there is grace. I have been blessed.

Hence for the other diagnoses along the way, I have adopted a philosophy of unfailing faith and knowledge that my body is truly amazing.

# About My Children

## CAROLE'S DAUGHTERS

My life is graced with three beautiful and gifted daughters.

My eldest daughter, Sue, is impassioned about her Lord and Savior, Jesus Christ, and the things of God. She has a love and tender heart for dogs, especially her miniature poodle Sadee. She relishes every moment spent at the ocean, tending to a garden, dancing, listening to music, and playing the guitar. It's virtually impossible for her to pass by a yard sale or antique store without stopping in to look for a great find. Sue is creative, loves decorating and making wherever she lives feel like home, as much as she enjoys all the preparation in entertaining family and friends in her eloquent and memorable style. She graduated from the University of Connecticut with a Bachelor of Science Degree in Marketing and is presently, and has been for many years, employed in the residential mortgage business.

My middle daughter, Dawn, enjoys a career in accounting. She spent four years in military service with the US Navy in California and Japan. It is meaningful to Dawn to have the opportunity to participate as a board member/volunteer with the 7th Regiment Drum & Bugle Corps, a non-profit organization that fosters a venue for young people drawn to the performing arts. She is passionate about mountain hiking, mountain biking, and dirt biking, with a new love for rock climbing. She can design and fashion a party in any theme with promises to be remembered for years to come. Dawn resides in Connecticut with her one son, Zachary, who is studying computer science engineering.

My youngest daughter, Cher, follows a career in dental assisting. She is the loving mother of four children, Ashley, Samantha, Mario, and Michael. She spends time supporting the ROTC program at the high school. Cher has creative talents in decorating and design. Young children and family pets are drawn to her innate quality to bring out their beauty and gentle spirit. It is a gift recognized by those who know her. She resides in Delaware with her husband, Jimmy, my wonderful son-in-law, a stepson, Josh, and her one son, Michael. Ashley and Samantha are pursuing a life in Vermont and Mario is in the air force soon to be joined by his brother, Mike.

Sadee and Susan

Zachary and Dawn

Samantha, Michael, Ashley, Mario, Jimmy, Cher, and Josh

# Twin Phenomena

The dictionary defines phenomenon as "1. any observable fact or event that can be scientifically described or 2. anything very unusual."

## MIRROR IMAGE

We have been defined as mirror image twins, which accounts for twenty-five percent of the one third of twins reported to be identical.

Mirror image means that there are certain features that actually mirror like a reflection—i.e., one using their left hand and the other using their right. This is one of the more quickly observed mirror images.

Carole was left-handed, and I am right-handed. Our mother tried adamantly to get Carole to use her right hand, which never completely worked. Today, Carole is ambidextrous.

In identical twins, these reflective images can be observed in hair cowlicks, birthmarks, and even internal organs.

For Carole and me, aside from the use of opposite hands, we have an amazing twin phenomenon that you will read about in the following account regarding birthmarks.

Other mirror images we are aware of are that we both have scoliosis, with the curvatures being in opposite directions. This condition can cause one leg to be longer than the other. For us, in keeping with the mirror image phenomenon, this facet is reflected on opposite sides.

If we were looking for other opposites, like our hair's natural parts being on opposite sides, I suspect there would be more mirror images to report that are not quite so obvious.

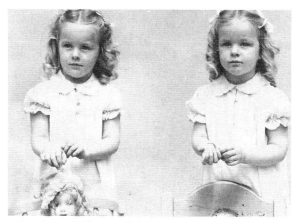

Carole and Elaine—Notice positioning of hands

Carole and Elaine

Elaine and Carole

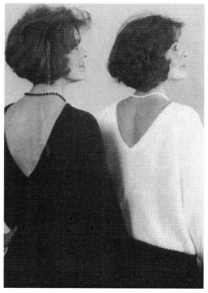

Elaine and Carole

# A BIRTHMARK

One of us has a birthmark—Carole. It is a flat little round circle on her right side, midway between her waist and underarm.

Where was mine? Why didn't I have one?

This factor helped give our parents reassurance as to who was who. For fourteen years, Carole had her special mark of identification. It took me fourteen years to catch up with my environmentally-made birthmark.

It was approaching dinnertime, and I was helping to set the table while my mother was cooking a pot roast. As the ingredients were browning a little too quickly, mom pulled the Dutch oven off the electric stove burner to slow the process, having no concept as to what was about to occur.

I was being "Miss Neatnick" reaching for the salt and pepper shakers on a shelf that was affixed over the stove. After all, why not rearrange the shelf a little and make it neater? Often I would make the attempt to get my mother's approval.

There I was, dressed in slacks, a blouse hanging out over the waist band, and my hair in rollers as I was going to a class party in the evening.

As I pulled away from the stove, having the shelf just as neat as I could make it, my blouse was in flames.

What ensued were screams and my mother calling out to me not to run as she grabbed me and tried to get me to roll on the braided rug my grandmother had made that was on the floor in front of the stove. Each time she tried to force me down on the rug, the flames were nearer my face, and at that moment, my strength prevailed.

When that didn't work, still calling out to me over and over again, "Don't run! Don't run!" she fortunately was able to maneuver me off the rug and pick it up so she could smother out the flames. It was a force against force. In those traumatic moments, mom had considered running for a coat or getting water from the sink nearby, anything to quench the flames, but felt certain if she let go of me, I would run. It would have been an unconscious response.

This was my first concern in life about survival, not only for myself, but also for my mother. It must have been difficult for me to grasp that she was okay, because I can still hear my questions. "How is my mother? Is she okay?"

While waiting for care, I also remember the odor of burnt/charred skin and wondering when relief would come. Would it come? Would I survive? Back then, they treated burns differently then they do today. I was swathed in Vaseline bandages that were held in place by ace bandages that encased my upper body and arms. They were changed frequently to try and prevent infection. The pain was such that I felt like I was in another place in time. Barely bearable!

This instance led to many months of nursing third degree burns, in semi-shock part of that time, and wondering if I would ever heal. Well, heal I did, amazingly so, considering the extent of the injury.

Carole was upstairs when this event occurred and said that our screams were so terrifying that she was too afraid to come down and see what was wrong. I can understand that feeling. By the time she mustered the courage, the event was winding down.

The phenomenon: I had one small scar on my *left* side the same size as Carole's birthmark on her *right* side, same point of location as if looking in a mirror.

I didn't miss having a birthmark that badly.

Could it be that mirror imaging was showing itself once again?

# FALSE LABOR

What is false labor? Can an identical twin have false labor?

It was a regular workday like any other until lunchtime. I had gotten a call that my mother and Carole were on their way out to lunch. There I was, wishing I could join them.

It wasn't an ordinary day, or an ordinary call, for Carole was expecting her first baby any day. She had just been to her doctor, and he had said she would have her baby before the end of that day. Had I heard right? They were on their way to lunch not the hospital?

At work, around 2:00 p.m., I started to feel kind of sick to my stomach to the point of making the decision to go home. This is probably a good point to mention that our family rarely gave in to an illness. Taking off from work was almost unheard of, yet home I went.

A call came that Carole was in the hospital. I was a mixed array of emotions… excitement to dismay. I could feel the disappointment slowly mounting as I realized I would not go to the hospital sick. There was no way I would take a chance of passing my illness on to Carole. How could I be sick right now when I wanted to be at the hospital with my sister and new niece or nephew? There I was, dealing with serious abdominal pains. This just couldn't be. There were nine previous months I could have been out of commission, but not now.

I don't remember the exact hour, somewhere around 5:00 p.m., but all of a sudden, I felt fine. Just like one had flipped a light switch. At that same moment, the phone rang and beautiful baby Susan had been born.

What do you think? Was that false labor?

What I know was that I got to see my beautiful new niece and Carole, the first to be a mother, that very evening. As we marveled at God's creation, I knew I would cherish my time of motherhood whenever it occurred.

However, for that moment I would derive much pleasure in being an aunt.

# Twin Things

---※---

## SAME CLOTHES

As much as we relished not dressing alike, it was not uncommon for us to find we had purchased the same item of clothing despite not shopping together. This brings to mind a specific occasion when my husband and I were going to a pool party and had invited Carole to join us.

As we dressed for the party, there we were with the exact same Rose Marie Reed leopard print bathing suits. Had they been simple in design and color, they may not have looked so identical. These leopard prints really made a statement, which was a step out of the box for both of us, but there we stood, Mike and Ike.

As if that weren't enough to add a little spice to the event, we decided that Carole would walk in with my husband and I would be the visiting sister. It is actually the only time I remember role-playing with each other. It really was not something we ever thought about doing. There was enough mixing up by outsiders without even trying. As we started this little charade, we became immediately uncomfortable and skipped the role-playing within twenty minutes of our impersonation.

What struck me at that event was that even though some friends were looking straight at me, they still were not certain that I wasn't my sister. I did not like that feeling.

Not only were a number of people confused as to which of us was my husband's wife, but one guest said she was so shaken that she was going home, leaving the party. She had identical twin granddaughters and was troubled by the confusion she felt. It was all "too much."

Years later, I had a touch of true empathy for those looking on at Carole and me. My brother-in-law married a woman who had identical twin daughters whose identity often confused me.

Ah ha, I said to myself, many times, "So this is what it feels like for those trying to tell us apart."

---

## UNIFORMS

When we went to private school for a brief, ever so brief period, we had to wear uniforms. Thus, we were dressed alike, but somehow that did not feel like we were dressing alike. I know that does not make perfect sense, but nonetheless that's the way it was. Perhaps the anonymity came from the fact we each made our own uniform due to economic considerations. Navy blue pleated skirts with two-pocket blazers defined the Mother of God Academy girls. Our creative sewing abilities guided us in producing the pattern and the finished product. However, within the identical context of fabric and design, we each knew our own stitching. Thus our uniforms took on their own unique statement that fostered our sense of individuality.

---

## DINNER DRAMA

There was an evening as young adults when Carole and I met for dinner at a local hotel restaurant. We met in the lobby. Where was the mirror? We didn't need one. When we looked at each other, we saw a clone. Black suits, black pumps, and red plaid wool scarves around our necks with the same flare. After a moment, one of us said, "Okay, which one is going home to change?" We settled for one removing her scarf before proceeding into the restaurant. Which one relinquished her scarf? You may have guessed it was the one with the outgoing personality who kept her scarf neatly in place. Right you are!

We were often amused when such happenings occurred as we had always put much emphasis on not dressing alike. Alas, once again!

---

## A DATE'S CONFUSION

Referring to clothing brings to mind a time when my date was coming to pick me up and I wasn't quite ready, so I asked Carole to answer the door and invite him in. This was not our first date. It certainly seemed like a natural enough thing to do. She obliged, dressed in jeans and a shirt.

My date shared with me that he looked at her and thought silently, "I can't believe Elaine is going out in jeans. I think I will have to change my plans." Back then, jeans were not as versatile as they are today.

It wasn't until I called to Carole from the room I was in down the hall, that my date realized Carole was not me.

---

## CHILDREN LOOK-ALIKES

Clearly, Carole and I did not like to dress alike, however, in many of our photos we often were, which was driven by our quasi modeling careers.

There is an interesting caveat here. While Carole and I made such an effort not to dress alike most of the time, we had an identical reaction to this twin thing.

Carole had three daughters and I had two sons. Would you believe she dressed her daughters alike and I dressed my sons alike? Literally *alike*. We did it unbeknown to each other… we lived miles apart. At one point, her oldest and my oldest asked us please not to dress them like their siblings. What were we doing? Sorry, Stephen! Sorry, Sue! Of course, your requests made perfect sense and were honored.

Stephen and Richard

Stephen and Richard

Richard and Stephen

Dawn and Susan

Susan and Dawn

## PARTIES: TO INVITE OR NOT TO INVITE

Too much attention? Is that possible? What kind of attention?

Carole and I had many friends from all the different cliques in Darien High School. After all, we had been raised to believe we should be friends with everyone. We did not look for differences in people, just in ourselves—very interesting as I now contemplate that.

We had also been told growing up that it was not necessarily a positive thing to be attractive. Quite the contrary, it could bring many problems your way. So I would find if someone referred to me as attractive it would be almost like I didn't hear it. I wanted to be pretty, I saw Carole as pretty, but yet that thought rested somewhere in the recess of my mind and got little attention.

I remember one day at school hearing about a party and a comment that I wasn't supposed to hear, "Don't invite the Sloan twins or the boys will give them all the attention." I was very troubled by that. It was somewhat like a confirmation of the fact that being attractive could be a detriment—particularly since there were two of us. There were many attractive young girls in Darien.

## FAMILY MIX UP

It was dinnertime when I arrived in Connecticut to visit my parents, Carole, and family. It was a visit I made just a couple times a year. As I walked into the kitchen, Carole was feeding her then youngest child in a highchair. Dawnie looked at me standing in the doorway about ready to take her next bite of food. However, the process came to an abrupt halt as she then looked back at her mother. She looked at me again and then back to Carole. Once more, we were both observed. Then came a scream that clearly said dinner was over.

I hurried out of the room in hopes that Dawnie would continue eating, but it wasn't going to be with Carole feeding her. Her little raised hand issued the order, not from you. She did finish eating after my father stepped into the mix. I found it interesting that such a young toddler knew what she needed to do to bring order to her universe, with a totally non look alike feeding her. From infancy to very early childhood, Dawnie was confused by our likeness more than the others. Following is another example.

---

## CONFUSING MOMENT

Another time, I went to visit Carole at her home and arrived early in the morning. She and I were in her room talking. Carole had walked out of the room for something and just moments later, Dawnie had gotten up and walked into her mom's room saying "Good morning, Mom." I announced, "Good morning, Dawnie, it's Aunt Elaine," at which point she looked at me and turned running back into her bedroom saying, "I can't stand it, I am going back to bed. I guess it doesn't matter." I felt bad for Dawnie, but didn't know how to make it better.

---

## IDENTICAL INTONATION

Many times over the years, our mother would want us to keep talking on the phone before she responded. It would take a while for her to determine who was calling. She often said the decision would come based on the content of the conversation and not by the voice. The intonation in our voices is so similar, it often confuses others and ourselves as well when heard on tape. Very similar mannerisms further add to the confusion and debate— Which one? Which one is it?

A time is recalled when we were working for affiliate companies each servicing some of the same accounts. A customer called in and was requesting information only to find he was talking to Carole and thinking it was Elaine.

He still comments on his confusion.

---

## YOUR RIB AND MINE

It was a perfect day to take my girls out to play. I told them if they took a quiet nap, I would take them out for the afternoon. Shortly after tucking them in, I decided I would do a couple of things around the house so that my time with them would not be cluttered with thoughts of things I had to do. Everything was moving along beautifully—me in my play clothes with a pair of clogs on my feet. I had one last thing to do and that was to take out the garbage. I was in very high spirits as I headed for the front door.

We were living in an apartment on the second floor. There were seven steps and a landing followed by another eight steps. I was kind of skipping down the steps with expectation of the afternoon with my girls. Just after turning the landing and making my way down the next eight steps, there I was in the air. My feet had slipped out from underneath of me and I came down flat on my back. The pain was excruciating, It took my breath away. My friend who lived in the next apartment heard me and ran to my aid. The result was three broken ribs. Unfortunately, I did not have the afternoon I wanted with my girls.

At that time, Elaine was living in Florida and I was living in Connecticut. I called her later that night after getting back from the hospital and we talked about what had happened only to find out that that very day she had fallen on the stairs and bruised her ribs. I guess misery does love company.

❧

## SAME CARDS

Now I know that most people believe that sending the same cards is purely a twin phenomenon, but I may be the one person along with my sister who is not certain. However, I guess you cannot argue with the many who think so when the numbers are so high. For years Elaine and I would send the same card to our sister or to our Mother or another.

Even more interesting, we would send the same card to each other. I would always pick a card that I thought would be perfect for Elaine. Many times on these special occasions when I would open a card that she had sent me, it was identical to the one I had just sent her.

Observing these events over the years, I would find that my sister Dawn, or maybe another in the family would have sent my mother the same card. However, I can say that my sister Dawn and I never sent the same card to each other.

Further, there have been times when someone close to the family will send the same card. I have thought perhaps it is an energy phenomenon, since all of life is an energy. What do you think?

---

## WHICH ONE IS MINE

Might a husband feel insecure being with a twin just by the nature of the phenomenon? Often, one of our husbands would express that he felt our allegiance was to each other, and he felt, on some level, in jeopardy in the relationship because of this. Nothing could have been further from the truth. Elaine and I could not have been more loyal to our respective partners. It was our nature. But there was nothing, *nothing*, we could do to sway their thinking. I am certain it came from outside influences. It came from those who thought they had a better handle on twins than the twins themselves. I know there were times their reactions to the sister-in-law were affected by where they were in their relationship with their wife. Yes, can you imagine that? It so amazed me when we grew up in a home that rarely ever mentioned the word twin and treated us so individually, how could this be happening in our married lives?

Compounded by these insecure feelings was the big mix up that happened from time to time. I used to feel sorry for our husbands when they would mix us up. I remember Elaine's husband walking into the kitchen and coming over to kiss her hello, only it was me. We were all having dinner at my home that evening. As he was just about to plant a kiss on my check while I was standing at the kitchen counter, I said, "I think you have the wrong one." In his dismay, he walked away saying, "I'll never get it right unless I am looking directly at you."

Now, I will say we do have the same mannerisms. I find them to be stunningly similar.

I used to watch Elaine, critique her style, because I would see myself, and decide if that was the way I wanted to do it. Actually, that was like having a front-row seat to see your own mannerisms.

※

## SOME ODDS AND ENDS

Another little twin thing is that Carole and I quite frequently find ourselves answering questions in unison, word for word.

On other occasions, we will stop the other one mid-sentence and say, "I know what you are going to say." Reply being, "Maybe you do and maybe you don't." Usually we do.

When growing up, I was told I was the reserved twin and Carole was the outgoing twin, like you had to be one or the other. We played those roles. What I later observed was when in a social setting without Carole being present, I was much more outgoing. Over the years I have garnered the self-confidence where I am no longer controlled by others' suggestions.

Example: years ago when I was working for a telecommunications firm, Carole came in to meet me for lunch not knowing that I had already left the office. Those in the office thought Carole was me and that I had had my hair colored at lunch time. As to "twin things," nothing significant has changed over the years. However, one thing still fascinates us. Even in periods where we have had decidedly different hair color, others still confuse us.

Just recently while Carole was grocery shopping, a friend of mine approached Carole to talk and did not realize it was not me despite the difference in hair color. At that period of time my hair was decidedly darker.

A tidbit—I recall a period when Carole and I tried to dress alike. Before going to bed we would decide on a particular outfit for the next day promising each other we would not change our minds. Invariably one or the other of us would awake with a change of heart. Individuality ruled.

# Picture Curiosity
# Can We Pique Yours?

---❦---

## IS THAT YOU OR ME? ELAINE OR CAROLE?

Of all our belongings, perhaps our photographs are our most prized possessions.

A good friend once said that a picture is simply a moment in time.

There have been a few moments over the years when we have had a picture taken separately and even together where we cannot identify ourselves wondering who is who?

What is interesting is when another looks and feels they can tell us apart and even then we are still not certain.

We'll leave it to you.

Which One?          Who?          Which One?

# The Sloan Sisters

---❦---

## MY SISTERS ELAINE AND CAROLE
### by: Dawn

Carole, Dawn, Elaine

"The girls" were the twins, my sisters. This was Mom's nickname for them. To me, they were Carole and Elaine, both then and now, even through the name changes. I rarely thought of them as twins. In our family, we were raised to have our own personal identity and the twins were no exception.

When the twins were born, we were living in a small town in Pennsylvania in one of about 30 to 40 row houses with three other sets of twins, all pre-school ages.

Mom was very pregnant. She couldn't even see her feet. Delivery day arrived a month early, and on March 20, 1941, the twins appeared in a hurry... Carole first and Elaine ten minutes later.

After a short stay in the hospital, a thinner mom came home with two little bundles. I stayed home with Aunt Adaire who was there to take charge. My job was to anticipate and wonder what it would be like to have two sisters. I had been an only child for 10 years and my life was about to change. It was exciting. However, the instructions were to look at, *not hold*, the babies until the proper way to hold them was learned... *no head bobbling* permitted. When they first came home, the girls were kept on the dining room table in hospital cardboard boxes/bassinets.

No bands played to announce their arrival home. Spring had arrived, as did Carole and Elaine swathed in blankets. It was a bright sunny and windy day. The challenge thrown to me was to become adept at knowing who was who. After a good hard look and close examination, I thought I had found the secret to each identity... Elaine had an oval shaped face, and Carole's was more round. A bright red, slightly raised birthmark donned Carole's chest. Mom did try to have it removed with radiation soon after the girls arrived home. Other than that, I saw no difference at that time.

Aunt Adaire, who had a no-nonsense personality stayed until our French Au Pair arrived a week later. All of a sudden, I had a plumpish, mild-mannered French mademoiselle to share my room and sleep in bed with me. Her job was to care for Mom, the twins, the house, and me. Once in a while, she permitted me to help push the twins in their baby buggy, and four of my closest friends haggled over taking their turns at pushing, too. When this occurred, I wanted to be the one chosen to go first but I had to be polite, because I had access to Elaine and Carole all the time. Mother felt that it wasn't my fault I now had sisters; therefore, I didn't have to care for them. Actually, I have wished through the years that Mom had given me more of a part in helping tend to my sisters.

Even as babies, each had a definite personality all their own. Mother encouraged it because she felt strongly that each person should be an individual. Individuality was the key for all of us. We heard many times, "No one can ask more from you if you do the best you can." Only Mom asked for more.

The twins were, as a rule, not dressed alike. One outfit I recall when they were dressed identically was when Mom and Dad collaborated on making coat outfits with matching bonnets in a bright plaid. They were around two years of age. Over the years, both girls made most of their outfits and, when purchased, each received the same thing usually in different colors. By the time they were fifteen, they were making most of their outfits.

Our father traveled a lot of the time when the twins were little. He worked in New York, leaving early in the morning and coming home late. It was decided that he would find a place that cut down on his traveling time. And he did. We moved to Plainfield, New Jersey, on a block close to the main thoroughfare and a block and a half away from one of the elementary schools. The house was in an area that Mom didn't like. However, the walls inside had pictures painted on them by the artist who had just moved out.

Here we were in a strange town, in an area whose school Mom felt was not what she wanted for me or her girls, no car, and two little three year olds.

Mom found another school a mile and a half away, cried on the principal's shoulder, and he made an exception for me to walk there each day. By the middle of the school year, we were on the road again to our new home on Maple Avenue in Metuchen, about ten miles away. Dad was away, the movers came, and Mom went with them. So I took my sisters, and off we scurried for a bus ride to our new home. I had been given instructions to "hang onto your sisters" and for them to hang on to me, so we began our journey to our new home on an unforgettable bus ride. And hang on to me the twins did! The third bus that came read *Metuchen*. It was ours. It was very crowded. We got on. No seats were available. What was I to do? The twins were three years old and had never been on a bus. No seats were found. People were standing. No one volunteered a seat. With two clinging little ones, I finally reached a pole that I could grab onto by a side exit. The bus started and stopped at least five times, challenging our footing. Unfortunately the emptying seats were filled before I could grab one of them. Finally we got one seat! I held one of my sisters and squeezed the other one between me and a sympathetic lady who just happened to get off at the next stop… another challenge! At last we had a "two for" for the three of us. Another thirty minutes brought us to our destination. We had arrived in Metuchen and were on our way to our new home.

Metuchen was where we stayed until my graduation from high school and completion of my first year of college at the New Jersey College for Women.

The twins and I attended Franklin School, grades K-12. The elementary school was on the ground floor on one side of the building and the secondary grades were spread across the top floor on the other side of the building. Once in school, the three of us rarely saw each other.

At the age of 16, and on a Christmas Eve, I met my husband to-be, Arthur. We began dating regularly. Sometimes we baby-sat my sisters. They always thought it was fun to hide and spy on Art and me. Usually they hid behind the sofa or around the corner at the top of the stairs. Their smothered giggling was always a give-a-way. Of course, we had to act surprised.

The years in Metuchen went quickly, and soon it was time for college. Unfortunately, the cost of college was beyond my family's means, and I commuted freshman year in a super 6 Essex to the New Jersey College for Women with Art and Jimmy, our friend, who owned the car. We always held our breath when we rolled down the hill that the engine would start or we would all be taking the train to New Brunswick. It usually started and off we'd go! Jimmy left me off at the Bee Hive, the commuter's campus haven. Then they drove across town to Rutgers University where they were both students. Mom and Dad insisted I take courses that would lead to a position when I graduated. Mom especially wanted all three of her daughters to go on to further education. Dad and Mom both thought I should be a teacher.

This was the year that my Mom and Dad went to Texas. I was invited to stay at Art's home, and Carole and Elaine went to stay with Aunt Margaret at Grandpa Sloan's farmhouse.

Dad's engineering firm, Peabody Engineering Corporation, moved most of its operations to the main corporate office in Stamford, Connecticut, and this meant Dad would be in the research and development department. It also meant we were on the move again. This time, we rented an old carriage house on Mansfield Avenue in Darien, Connecticut, close to where Dad worked.

Our new neighbors who lived in front often invited us for miniature golf on a course in their back yard that my Dad designed for them, and we invited them back for horseshoes. I worked at Peabody's during the summers and shared the large bedroom that stretched across the front of the house with my kid sisters who were, then, around nine. The three of us helped Dad with digging a basement for the carriage house, and Art painted the carriage house.

The next three years, I lived on campus, coming home for holidays and summers. The twins were growing up. I became engaged the June I graduated Douglass College; New Jersey College for Women had become a part of Rutgers University.

Art and I were planning a November wedding, and I wanted my sisters to be in the wedding. They were only twelve so I asked them to be my junior bridesmaids and proceeded to select gowns that had the sophistication for my bridesmaids and yet also for my junior bridesmaids.

In the next few years, my family was on the move again to Pleasant Street, next to an apartment in Stamford, and finally, they bought their Bonnybrook Road home in West Norwalk. Art and I visited monthly from the time we were married until our children became involved with activities that were scheduled on weekends.

By this time, my sisters were young adults. During those years and ever since, we have shared concerns with each other and have been supportive, distance permitting. Carole has always had the tendency and tenacity to make her points heard by Mom and Dad and most times won them. Elaine made her points but most times would let her sister do the talking. She is more reserved, and she will push her point only so far. The girls are independent thinkers and their own persons. They both are caring and supportive of each other.

There is only one other difference, and that is in the religion area. I was baptized a Methodist, attended a variety of churches—whichever one that was closest to where we lived—confirmed at the age of 12 in the Presbyterian Church, married in the Dutch Reform Church, and after I was married, became an Episcopalian. I still attend the Episcopal Church. Mother never shared her beliefs or her religious background with us. She did insist we should all go to church. Elaine and Carole were confirmed Episcopalians even though today they attend different churches and their beliefs differ from each other. We all believe in God. Episcopalians believe that God is the Father, Jesus Christ is the son, and our soul is the Holy Spirit. This differs from non-Christian religions, because many of the others believe that Jesus was an Apostle/missionary and not the son of God born of the Virgin Mary. Throughout the story, note the descriptions expressed by each twin and how they differ in their manner of expressing themselves based on their beliefs, ideas, and personalities.

How people express themselves and how they approach life often tells "volumes about them." An old adage, "Action speaks louder than words," also is another way to learn about people.

Yet another way is the actual voice—if not in person, then via the telephone. For me, this is one area where it is hard to know which twin is speaking. Their voices often sound the same. However, if I listen carefully and wait long enough, ninety-nine per cent of the time either the voice or the context of what they are saying will be the key to who is on the other end of the line.

The twins are identical by definition. At times, it is hard to tell them apart *and* there is no doubt that, despite their likenesses and differences, they are both individuals in identity, looks, and personality, yet they are attuned to each other. Each has her own charm; both are supportive, caring, and loving individuals. Does it sound like I love my sisters? I do. Each has a mind of her own. They are not followers but usually team players.

As the years go by, there is a closeness among the three of us. And for Carole and Elaine, "twiny" is only a word for those without *individuality*.

<hr/>

## SISTER DAWN
### *by: Elaine*

It is often said that the first born in a family is the greatest achiever. Dawn certainly was one for Carole and me to look up to and feel proud of as we grew to understand her talents. What a role model!

Dawn excelled! She had her own column in the local newspaper as a sports reporter through her high school years in Metuchen, New Jersey. She was in the drama club, was a convincing actress, enjoyed modern dance, and was an outstanding student chosen to represent New Jersey for Girls Nation. I know I have missed something, but those are the accolades from my memory bank.

And she was so pretty with her long, pageboy, engaging smile and great shape. I remember looking at pictures of her and thinking, *Might I someday look like Dawn?*

I loved when Dawn would babysit for us on very rare occasions. Carole and I would hide behind the sofa in the living room to surprise her and Arthur, her special beau. Looking back, I am certain they knew we were there and just played along with us.

When they got married, I was so excited about having a good looking and nice brother-in-law. The fact that I was going to be a junior bridesmaid in their wedding was almost surreal. Thank heavens I was old enough. To think that I would be wearing a gown in a wedding at such a young age was elating. The gown was peacock blue with a velvet top, strapless with netting over the shoulders and netting over long satin skirts. What a day! Carole and I were so excited.

Dawn and Art's first home was in Metuchen, New Jersey. I felt a sense of awe as I would enter their apartment and look around at all their decorating. I liked it. Here was my sister, older yes, but my sister, moving into her own home. I was bold enough to feel it was kind of mine, too—at least another little haven in my world.

Dawn and Art lost their first baby, and I thought that was about the saddest thing that could ever happen. I was so proud when I became an aunt when Douglass was born and an aunt again when Daryl Beth was born—two remarkably adorable babies, who have grown into remarkable adults. Daryl added to our family tree two very successful children, a daughter, Katee, and a son, Brian.

Dawn brought certain realities into my life and probably the most significant was making me aware that when ready to enter college I would need to be solely responsible for the cost, as she had been. As much as my mother promoted the importance of education finances were never mentioned. If my parents had had the money, there would have been no question, but that wasn't the fact. They had made sure during our elementary and high school years that we were in a good school district and insisted on us taking only academic courses. In any regard, college came later.

In the earlier years, I would say that Dawn was somewhat like a mother figure to me. Recently, I have read a couple letters I had written while my parents were in Texas and Carole and I were staying with our aunt. As I was reading one of these letters, it felt like it would have been meant for my mother, but in checking the salutation reaffirmed it was meant for Dawn.

Dawn has been so caring and generous with me during my life, in a way that has touched me deeply. And I have valued our many hours of conversation sharing intellectual insights as well as happenings within our life's arenas.

There is one threesome comparison I would like to make. Carole and I have always enjoyed entertaining, small or large groups, creating some memorable events. However, our sister Dawn is the epitome of a great entertainer from A to Z, creating the perfect atmosphere and preparing the best foods that cling in your memory for years. All she does is impeccably plan and execute no matter how small or large the event.

Over the years, our relationship has evolved into that of friends as well as sisters, with much love and companionship. I treasure that.

## SISTER DAWN
### by: Carole

What I know is that everyone should have a sister, Dawn. She is kind, caring, loving, compassionate, and smart coupled with practicality and a sense of humor—a sister, a friend, and an occasional second mom.

When I think of my earlier years, the first vivid picture that comes to me is when Dawn was going to her high school prom. I thought she was pretty as a picture. I still remember her powder-blue moire gown she wore and her beautiful pageboy hair that fell just to her shoulders. I don't know if she was voted prom queen, but if she wasn't she should have been. Somehow, in the recess of my mind, I see a picture of her and the banner said, "A Pretty Girl is Like a Melody." If this actually existed, it was no mistake. She was sadly ten years older than Elaine and me so we didn't have a lot of time with her. I would have really liked that!

When Elaine and I were coming out of elementary school, she was going into college. This gives perspective to our age difference. In the earlier years, Mother did not want my sister Dawn to have to feel like the twins were her responsibility, so Mother did the major part of taking care of us. I have come to find out in talking with my sister, she would have liked it to be a little different, too. Dawn has always had this sweet loving and generous spirit. That has never changed.

Over the years, we have developed a relationship that has surely made up for anything missed back in the early days. I do however have a recollection of early days but not as vivid—just an awareness that she was there being her loving self. I always felt happy when we did have some time together. I do remember her presence when we were moving into Metuchen and the bus ride and it felt reassuring to have her there. She was a comfort!

I have often wondered if the move to Maple Avenue wasn't part of the grand design so she would meet Arthur later to become her husband and the father of her two beautiful children, Daryl Beth and Doug. They were the sweetest little kids, and Elaine and I had our first taste of being aunties. We were so proud.

I remember going to Dawn and Art's apartment after they were just married and visiting. On one occasion she had us to a Spanish rice dinner. She used to say it was the one dish she knew how to cook. It was really good. I loved my sister, and visiting with her was a delight.

We were nine years old when we moved to Connecticut and sadly left Dawn behind to go off to college. There was a space for her in our new bedroom that Elaine and I shared. Her visits would fill the air with great excitement.

When Dawn and Art married, Elaine and I were so excited about being in her wedding. I still remember the gowns we wore. They were really so beautiful with this peacock blue velvet top and tulle skirts. I can still see Dawn with this gorgeous lace, long-sleeved gown with sweet pea buttons up the front and a veil that was attached to a specially designed cap that fit her hair perfectly. She was a vision!

As the years went by, we gratefully grew closer, for we had more in common. We were all married with children, and our lives took on a new flavor. Time together brought cherished moments.

Later on, I enjoyed several vacations to the eastern shore in Maryland, where Dawn and Art had a beautiful home on the water. It was lovely, and the time spent there so enjoyable. Dawn and I would spend time in St. Michaels touring the little shops and purchasing special mementos of a glorious time. I felt like queen for the week, and this was no surprise if you only knew my sister, Dawn. Truly important to me, over the many years, are the phone calls we have shared to support each other by listening with compassion and the laughter when sharing joyous moments from afar.

I will never forget the phone call I received from my niece that my sister was in the hospital and it was serious. My heart sank, and for the first time, I caught a glimpse that she could be gone. I immediately went into prayer and asked God not to let her go. With His Grace, she is alive and living near me for the first time in sixty years. This is a beautiful thing, and I am so thrilled and so blessed. Amen.

Dawn's and Art's wedding party

Dawn and Art's daughter's wedding
Dawn, Doug, Daryl, and Art

Dawn's high school graduation picture

Elaine's high school graduation picture

Carole's high school graduation picture

# What Our Children Have To Say

———— ❧ ————

## SLOAN'S CHILDREN
### *Stephen Shares*

What is it like having a mother who is a twin? Remember the Wrigley's Doublemint Chewing Gum commercial, featuring identical twins, with the slogan "Double the pleasure, double the fun with Doublemint gum"?

There were lots of doubles as I remember. On occasion, I would get the same birthday card from both my mother and my aunt. One time, they bought the same car in the same color. The only difference was the model year. They both thought they had the greatest car.

Double the fun can also be double the frustration. There were times that I remember looking at my mom and aunt sitting in the same room and doing a double take to figure out which one was my mom; hoping one would speak so I would know. As I got older I could usually tell them apart just by looking at them, yet when talking on the phone I would need to let the conversation go on for a few minutes before I would be sure it was my mom on the other end of the line. My mom had a different tone when she spoke. My aunt had a slight New England accent that my mother had lost over the years.

Just this year, I took my mom to a party at the home of a work colleague of mine. Shortly after we arrived, a man walked up to my mom saying, "Hi, Raina. How are you?" My mom, Sloan, never having met the man and not expecting to see someone she knew, just looked at him. She had a look on her face suggesting utter confusion. We came to find out he was someone with whom my aunt had a work relationship. That was not the first time and probably won't be the last that something like that happens.

As twins, my mom and aunt share the same birthday... this is usually not the case for most siblings. However, my dad and his brother shared the same birth date, only five years apart. Though my dad and uncle were not identical in looks or in personality, they have very similar sounding voices, make the same type of comments, and have many of the same values. My mom and aunt did look very much the same at times, but they were, in many ways, more individualistic than my Dad and Uncle.

## Richard Shares

Growing up the son of an identical twin was more fascinating to me than it was difficult.

The areas that interested me the most were their appearance, the genetic factor and their ability to be best friends while still having some of that sibling rivalry.

I know that siblings can be close, but it always seemed to me that my mother and aunt treated each other more as best friends than as sisters. I compare this to my relationship with my brother, and while I love my brother and respect him for all that he has become, I don't see our relationship as a best friend type of relationship. I remember being a young kid, hearing my mother discuss things with my aunt that are the types of things I discuss with my friends but not my brother. I have known a few other twins, and it seems like they are able to connect more than the normal siblings might connect. It was interesting to see my mother and aunt so close but still be able to have that sibling rivalry that is similar to what my brother and I shared growing up. I don't know if it is a twin issue or the fact that they grew up sharing so much together because they were the same age in the same house that allowed them to have this type of relationship, but it seems very different than what I see most siblings sharing.

I always found my mother's and aunt's looks to be fascinating. As identical twins, you would think they would look a lot alike and might be hard to tell apart. I found this to be true more as a young kid than I do as an adult. I don't think this was because I became more aware of their differences, making it easier to tell them apart, as much as it was that they seemed to go through cycles where they would look more alike at times than others.

I saw pictures of them as kids, and I know they looked very much alike. But I think, as they grew up and moved onto their own families, they developed more of their own identity. At times, it was as if they shared the same brain and got very similar hairstyles, even though they were miles apart and to my knowledge had never discussed the hairstyle prior to getting it done.

I do find it very interesting to visit and see just how much they can still look alike even though they have lived apart for so many years. I have often wondered if they plan some of this to confuse people, or if they are just connected somehow by being identical twins that allows them to share their thoughts. Is it from spending so much time together growing up that allows them still to have similar tastes many years later, or could there be some sort of genetic connection that maybe only a set of twins really shares?

Going through Biology in high school, I enjoyed learning about genetics, and how it work. Because of this, I find it fascinating that, my mother and aunt are identical twins. It genetically makes my brother and me half-brothers to my cousins. I certainly understand this is only a genetic issue. I find this fact can create quite an interesting conversation. I know I have had some very interesting and philosophical conversations about the truth of this fact. Growing up, I really thought it was a cool fact, now I just enjoy a fun conversation about it with someone who cares enough to take up the issue.

---

## CAROLE'S CHILDREN
### *Susan Shares*

Carole, Sue and Elaine

The third twin minus 20? As the eldest child of the "Sloan Twins," bearing a striking resemblance to mom and to my aunt, I have been afforded a rare glimpse of what the life of an identical twin might be like and the benign confusion that often ensues from displaying very similar physical characteristics.

At the close of Christmas services a few years back at my Aunt Elaine's church, (mind you, I had only attended services there one other time) a young girl standing at the rail of the balcony caught my eye. She was all of 8 or 9 years old, staring straight into my eyes, was offering an eager, full arm wave "hello," accompanied with a grand smile that stretched from ear to ear. Having no previous connection to the sweet young lady, I realized in a moment that she must have thought I was my aunt. I returned her greetings, nodded my head, and smiled to her and to myself.

The story doesn't quite end here. As our exchange of pleasantries was concluding, my aunt walked over to me to say something. I shared the case of the mistaken identity with my aunt; we both chuckled and looked to the balcony to see which little girl we had confused. Well, she was still standing there, now with a rather perplexed gaze, looking at me, then to my aunt, back to me, back to my aunt, and so on until we all again greeted one another from afar with smiles and waves. Finally she was resolved that there were two.

Seconds later, my mom emerged as well to talk with my aunt and me. I couldn't help stealing a look to the balcony for the young girl, thinking of how she might be processing what she was seeing now. Her face displayed a question mark that was larger than life. How could this be… three? Unimaginable, utterly perplexed! A final wave and smiles abound and we were all on our way. I can only imagine that my mom and my aunt experienced this mistaken identity for the whole of their lives.

During our early years, there were many more "twin" moments where mom and Aunt Elaine would arrive at a family gathering in the same outfit; send us the same birthday card on the same birthday; buy the same car within days of each other, or sport the very same hair style, color and look at the same time. Were these mere coincidences or was there a "twin" thing going on? Our two families rarely lived in close proximity so we always asked about any pre-visit planning between my mom and aunt. In every case, their answer was a resounding no. I seem to recall there was a time or two that even the "twins" were amazed by the similarity or identical nature of their choices. It is fair to say that there is a picture, or two, or three where the true identity of the subject remains a mystery. Hum… Is it Carole or Elaine? We all voice an opinion looking for the smallest detail to render a decision, but to no avail. None of us, including the twins, is really 100 percent sure.

All in all, I was seldom confused by the *who's who* of the "Sloan Twins." I think children are quite adept at recognizing their own mom even when there's an aunt who looks just like her. Those outside the family seemed far more enamored with the idea of identical twins and posed far more questions about what life was like and the ease of telling them apart. My friends would often lament that they could not distinguish between the two.

For all us, though taking liberties of speaking for my sisters (Dawn and Cheryl) and cousins (Stephen and Richard), life was like any other typical family… until it was time for a visit! We would all get together for the bigger holidays and some school vacations. The anticipation of my cousins' arrival was almost too much to bear, especially when we were younger. Stephen, the oldest child of my aunt and two years behind me, was my best, closest friend in the whole world. And as the story goes we were inseparable for the duration. My younger sister, Dawn, and Stephen's younger brother, Richard, were also close in age and shared a similar companionship. It was Steve with Sue and Dawn with Richie, off playing together, stirring up trouble, or creating some magical world. It was a natural fit for us all. Were these tight knit kinships an uncanny phenomenon of being born to and raised by identical twins, or were they purely the result of good, strong, family bonds found among many families? I think the latter.

What does set us apart, is when I learned that genetically speaking, the "girls" and the "boys" (as we were fondly referred to), being born to identical twin moms, are actually biological half brothers and sisters to each other! This concept was and is, more fascinating to me than the fact that our moms are identical twins. Five kids and two moms have a special genetic bond that does make us different. Maybe it does shed some light on why we were all so close. The concept of having two half-brothers with a different mother *does*, at the very least, make us rather unique and set us apart from the average family. For me (and this descriptive is truly from my heart) the genetic connection is the "coolest" part.

When Mom came to me and asked if I would share my thoughts about what life was like being born to and raised by an identical twin parent, I was hesitant at first. I had really never given it very much consideration. At first glance, life really didn't, in any way, seem extraordinary. What might I say that would be of interest, uniqueness, or importance about being the child of an identical twin? Through times of contemplation and prayers for guidance, I fondly remembered much. Some of which has already been shared. I was also harkened back, given a small glimpse into the tender heart of remembering what life looked like through the eyes of a five year old.

*I was the luckiest little girl in the whole wide world. My mom was so beautiful. I recall seizing every opportunity to show her off to my friends, classmates, and teachers. I wanted everyone in my world to know just how lovely she was. Moreover, I had something even better. What was the icing on the cake? My mom was an identical twin, and I couldn't wait to share that I had an aunt who looked just like her! Imagine that! I was the luckiest little girl in the world.*

Today, the Sloan twins are as distinctive and individual as any two sisters are. Their style, life pursuits, and personality are uniquely their own. They do not dress alike, wear the same hairstyle, or follow the same path. Yet their voice inflections, mannerisms, and intrinsic facial characteristics remain unmistakably identical. And yes, they are still undeniably beautiful.

## Dawn Shares

Even though my mom was a twin, I can't really think of too many things growing up that made it seem like my mom was different than anyone else's.

When I was young, I do remember when my aunt would come and stay with us for the holidays, that it was hard to tell who was who in the morning (they looked a lot alike to me). So I would wait until something happened that gave away who was who, it could be content of conversation, the laugh, something small. And I would take note of what they were wearing and that is how I would identify them "quickly" for the day. Of course for any type of personal one on one interaction I did not need to rely on the clothing to tell.

I would say by the time I hit middle school (that would put them at around their early 30's), their faces started to change from each other, and it became much easier to tell them apart.

Unless someone else brought it up or asked me about it, it never really crossed my mind. I don't recall too much emphasis being placed upon them being twins. They didn't really dress alike, and to me, they had very different personalities.

It was so matter-of-fact for us that, when I was asked to write this, it was the first time I had really been exposed to the "twin phenomenon" and how much people think about this as being special or different. To me, it just happens that my mom and aunt have spent years looking a lot alike and with some similarities, which seem to be diminishing greatly as they get older.

I would say they are very different people and are no more alike to each other, than I am to my sisters (except in appearance).

## *Cher Shares*

When asked to write what it was like growing up with my mom as a twin, I felt puzzled. Actually, this is the first time I have ever thought about it. There really was no significant impact on me as to my mom being a twin. My mom was my mom and my aunt was my aunt. Just like any other family!

In thinking about this now, I have to say the only times it would personally stump me and make me ask myself, "Who is who?" is in one scenario of answering the phone. We did not have caller ID back growing up and sometimes it would take a sentence or two before I realized to whom I was speaking. And if we didn't have caller ID now, I would still be stumped for a few moments. And another scenario: looking at old photos. I remember sometimes my mom and aunt struggling to guess who was who.

I feel the biggest responses came from the outside world. When I would have friends over, they would be awestruck at my mom and aunt's similarities. Or being out in public, people would stop and do a double take to make sure their eyes weren't playing tricks on them. It was like watching a tennis match with people's eyes going back and forth sometimes. It was fun to watch.

Yet, for me, besides the occasional humor in people's reactions, it felt no different having a mom who is a twin. I grew up knowing and having a relationship with both of them individually, and with that bond, it was easy to see each of them as they are: my mom and my aunt!

# POEM BY CHER

TWINS...
Twins is what my nana was told
Not one girl but two girls
For you to hold

IDENTICAL...
Gene for Gene the same they are
Two girls to become women
This will turn heads near and afar

FEATURES...
God would equip
Same eyes, same nose, same ears, and lips
Mesmerizing to those who see
Yet looking at my sister, I don't see me

TRAITS...
Their voices and laughter carry a similar tone
Uncanny to most who hear
Especially when talking to them on the phone

CHARACTERISTICS...
This is where the difference lies
As we are not the same
At least I don't see me, in my sister's eyes

TWINS...
Yes, we are to be seen
There are many differences in between
We are not one, we are two
When you look at us and we look back at you.

# Different Perceptions and Twin Events

Most siblings share happenings within their early years. This is more the norm than not. We were no exception, except we shared them from perhaps what one might call a closer vantage point. Despite that closer vantage point, what has proven interesting at times is how differently we perceived a happening.

You will note that the following events are written from either our individual perceptions or from a shared view.

## GRANDMOM DEAN
### *by: Elaine*

There is nothing like a grandmother. How do I know that? I am one, and it is one of life's most extraordinary experiences.

We visited infrequently my father's mother; she died when I was very young. My only recollection of her was sitting in a recliner type chair in her bedroom, which even as a child I remember seeming dreary. The terms they used were diabetes and dropsy. I don't ever remember seeing her other than in her chair and often doing jigsaw puzzles. To give you some idea of the absence of relationship, unfortunately, I do not even remember what Carole and I called her.

My maternal grandmother, I called "Grandmom." When we visited, we would often spend the night, and I would always look forward to my grandmom combing and braiding her silvery waist-length hair each morning. How did one's hair ever get that long? As she artfully twirled her hair in a neat bun I contemplated, Could it be she never had a haircut? *And* she used to wrap her toes before putting on her oxford styled shoes that had a slight heel. I don't think they even make that style any longer. This latter ritual was one that piqued my curiosity. However, as much as I questioned things, I never asked her why.

Grandmom loved violets! When you walked into her home, which she shared with an aunt, who never married, you entered a sun parlor with windows on three sides. Along the whole length of the windowsill were beautiful violets, all colors. They always caught my attention for they looked so perfect—loved, one might say. I wonder if that is why I was so drawn to Bonwit Teller's trademark image of purple violets with their vibrant green leaves on a white background. Bonwit Teller's has been out of business for many years, and to this day, I still have some special lingerie with their famous design. I knew nothing of Bonwit Teller's when years earlier I made my tenth-grade prom dress in a fabric with like-pattern that caught my attention. One of my girlfriends liked it so much I gave it to her to wear to the prom.

I really looked forward to the special treats grandmom would have, wonderful pastries and pies! In our home we never had desserts. Diabetes ran in our father's family and my mother's way of protecting us was not to have sugar in our diets. Looking back I remember my very first coke was at a birthday party of a friend when I was in the sixth grade. Oh, that coke, I thought it was so so good.

The recollection that stands out most about my grandmom Dean was when we went to visit she always had a special treat for

Carole and me. My grandmother was about 5' 1" tall, with a bit of a tummy and a glint in her hazel green eyes. Now, this special treat would be delivered by her standing before us with her hands behind her back and asking us to choose which hand we wanted. Each hand held an alike item except for perhaps a difference of color. I remember feeling the curiosity of how she got from point A with no treat in hand to point B, standing before us with treats without my seeing the transition.

This wonderful little dramatic moment, created a mix of emotion, for my grandmom always had Carole choose first. It wasn't that Carole asked to choose first and she let her, it was that grandmother saw to it that Carole had the first choice. I never understood that. Carole said it was because my grandmom felt I was the favorite twin and this was her way of making things more even.

The only way I can respond to that is to say I would not have said there was a favorite twin except when my grandmom handed out her treats. If I was a favorite with my parents, I cannot tell you how that manifested, I haven't a clue. I didn't then and I still don't.

While you would think that sounds fair and fine, perceptions matter and this made me want to cry, but I didn't. I loved my grandmother anyway. Other than our little painful good-bye ritual, visits would be somewhat enjoyable.

My first son, Stephen was born shortly before my grandmom passed away and she was so delighted she got to see him. Her words, "I got to see my Stephen." I liked that she was so excited about his birth.

Grandmom Dean

*by: Carole*

Lily. That is my grandmom's name. I say it because she is alive in my heart. I loved grandmom and so wish I could have known her better. On our infrequent visits to see her it was always exciting. There is just something about going to see your Gram. Grandmom spent much of her time helping the Salvation Army and playing bingo there. When she would win something she would have such delight giving her treasures to her little grand girls. My sister, Dawn when she was younger and then Elaine and me.

Grandmom, would hold these treasures one in each hand behind her back, and she would always ask me to pick first. Somehow, even as a young child, it felt uncomfortable to me and I would say, "Grandmom why do I have to go first?" She would reply, "Because you are not the favorite." (This I had always felt, but her words were bittersweet. They confirmed to me what I felt, and it hurt, but I knew she also cared enough about me to make it different somehow.) I would every now and again ask Elaine for her treasure and hold it behind my back with mine and have her pick a hand and this made me feel better, because I loved my sister and didn't want her hurt too.

Grandmom lived in a big house on a corner with a great wrap-around yard and the prettiest weeping willow tree where we would enjoy playing. There was an ice cream store diagonally across the street; always a highlight of our visits. Frequently we would go over to the corner store to buy ice cream for our after dinner treat. The anticipation of our dessert made up for the uneasiness at dinner. The rooms were big and I can remember everyone sitting around the large dining room table for meals, but it seemed to be a quiet time. Later I learned that when grandpop came to dinner he felt kids should be seen and not heard, hence it became a way of life for the family from early on. I don't remember him much except sitting in his overstuffed chair listening to the radio. I believe he was a respected business man in his day…in plumbing and heating.

One day Elaine and I were playing upstairs and running down the hall. Well I kept going and didn't stop until I ended up falling into the radiator. Since Mother had left us for a brief time with grandpop I remember him taking a sheet and cutting it up and wrapping a piece around my head to control the bleeding until my mother came home to take me for stitches. Otherwise, he said nothing. He was tall and thin with a mustache, and I often wondered why he never said much—that was that.

After grandpop died, grandmom and her eldest daughter moved in a row home next door. So we would visit her there. Aside from those cherished visits my last recollection of grandmom was when she was sick and we went to see her. They had her in a hospital bed in the dining room and I remember looking at her thinking, *How beautiful my grandmom looks.* To me she didn't look sick, although I knew differently. I just didn't want her to be. I remember her white hair that looked like spun silver pulled back; and her skin had an unusual glow I did not remember seeing before. She looked just like an angel. I still see her just like that and I always will for it is the sweetest of memories.

I do not remember clearly my other grandmom on my father's side. Her name was Louisa. We did not visit often and I don't think we had much of a relationship. Looking back it feels really sad to me and I am not certain how that happened. But it did. I wish it could have been different.

## MISS HALLOWELL'S DANCE CLASS
### *by: Elaine*

We tripped the light fantastic.

To be included in Ms. Hallowell's dance class was considered quite special. It was an exclusive class by special invitation and required its participants to wear white gloves.

I thought Miss Hallowell was the most feminine graceful lady as she twirled around the dance floor in her beautiful chiffon dress with her clicker denoting the exact moment either boys or girls would cross the dance floor in pursuit of a partner for the next dance.

We met at one of the local churches, and within the auditorium, chairs were arranged in two lines facing each other from across a large room. Girls sat on one side, and boys on the other. When the clicker sounded, by direction, either boys or girls would dart across the room to pick their partner for the next lesson. There was nothing dainty or refined about that moment. Always a few hoped not to be left sitting, as the count was never exact.

I always hoped for the "right" one to ask me to dance, as I wondered who it would be. Of course there was always those "oh, no" moments as you anxiously awaited to be chosen. Even if it was girl's choice, it did not mean you would reach your preferred destination before someone else. This little ritual had a lot to do with my interpretation of the evening.

I don't remember Carole and me ever sitting next to each other in the great lineup. It was not planned that way consciously, but maybe subconsciously. Nevertheless, had I been making a conscious decision, it would have looked the same. That would have felt like a contest I would not have enjoyed. By that time, we were well on our way to experiencing individual events.

There was a time I was making a green corduroy skirt for dance class, which was later that evening. The corduroy was so fine that it looked and felt just like velvet. I really liked it, except I was having a problem putting in the zipper. Well, my father arrived home early enough to finish the task so that I could wear my new skirt that evening. I loved that skirt and loved that my father had dexterity!

Miss Hallowell's dance class did not end for any of the reasons one might expect. One evening, the boys in our dance class decided they were going to pick up Miss Hallowell's "cute" beetle car and move it from the street onto the lawn somewhere away from the road. That was it: the end of Miss Hallowell's dancing class. There was no more wondering if I would be left sitting after everyone else was chosen to trip the light fantastic.

I took something special with me from that dance class. The waltz with the grapevine was my favorite step next to the lindy. Over the years, I have enjoyed dancing a great deal. Interestingly when the twist appeared with partners dancing separately I was at a loss. This always felt a little showy to me. I much preferred being held and led by my partner... Miss Hallowell style.

## by: Carole

To live in Darien was to know of Miss Hallowell's dancing school. Notice I said to know of, because if you were not in the "in crowd"—the more elite of Darien—most likely, you would not be receiving an invitation to attend. At that time, I was old enough to know it was a blessing to be there, but as I look back, I think it was absolutely stuffy. There were maybe twenty-five little girls dressed in their Sunday best and twenty-five little boys dressed in suits. We all wore white gloves. We met in the social room of the local Congregational Church on the Green. There were chairs neatly lining the room, and the girls sat on one side and the boys on the other. Then in the center of the room was the lovely Miss Hallowell. She looked just like Ginger Rogers to me, but I wouldn't go so far as to say her partner looked like Fred Astaire. We all aspired to be something that would resemble this beautiful duo.

Miss Hallowell had this little clicker in one of her gloved hands that she would click to get attention or to herald the opportunity to scurry across to the other side of the room to pick a partner. I loved girls' choice, because when it was boys' choice, this little boy, the shortest in the class, would run over and choose me, the second tallest girl. I say next to the tallest because

I believe my twin was slightly taller. I used to ask, "Why do you pick me, Billie?" He said it was because he thought it looked cute. As I was resting my chin on the top of Billie's head, I couldn't help but wonder how this could possibly look cute.

On girls' choice, I ran as far away from Billie as I could so as not to give him false hope when he saw the rush of girls coming across the floor. I had to run fast to be sure that I reached someone before I was left standing alone with Billie. Now I knew this could happen, because on rare occasions, it did. Don't get me wrong. Billie was a great kid, just not a great dance partner—as you can envision.

After several years, the class started rebelling about having to attend. On this one particular night, all the kids went outside and enveloped Miss Hallowell's little yellow VW bug. Yes, they picked it up and moved it to the center of the church lawn. It wasn't long after that that we all said goodbye to Miss Hallowell's dancing school.

Always in the recess of my mind were my memories of Miss Hallowell as I was growing up, and gratitude for that experience. I remember my junior and senior years in school and dancing with my boyfriend. We would enter the dance contests at the local country clubs and always placed in the top three. The waltz and lindy were our two favorites. I thought the grapevine step was so majestic. It made me feel that I was untouchable at those moments. I felt like I was on a cloud. (I believe that is what one calls enchanted.) In my adult years, on a rare occasion, I would think, *I wonder what it would have been like to be one of Billie Rose's long stem beauties.*

My dancing days ended, and it was not uncommon to see me dancing around my home with a broom. Yes, the broom was my frequent partner when music would be playing, and my memories of those good old days came streaming back to me. Ah… dancing!

# ALL ABOUT HARRY
## *by: Carole*

I will never forget Harry. He was quite prominent in our later teen years. He had this undying crush on my sister. She did not return the favor with the same fervor. That was apparent to everyone but Harry. As my mother would say, he had a bad case of "Hope Springs Eternal."

It was commonplace for Harry to show up at the door with his "geetar" tucked under his arm, ready to croon to the family with hopes that Elaine would show up while he was doing his thing. I need to say that he serenaded in coffee shops once in awhile so he wasn't half-bad, and on some level mother loved his appearances. You see Elaine had some other interests and poor Harry was not at the top of the list.

Often, Harry would turn to me and say, "I guess I could take you out." Not wanting to be a second fiddle, I would tell him that was okay; he could wait. Elaine and I talked about this and thought I should take him up on his offer sometime. Little did I know…

This one afternoon, while we were cruising around in his classy convertible with the top down, enjoying the day, Harry suggested going for a plane ride. Unbeknownst to the family and surely to me, he had a pilot's license for a piper cub. Being young and maybe foolish, I said, "Let's go." As I climbed into the second seat of the two-seater, my heart did an appropriate flip-flop. After his vow not to fly too high, off we went into the wild blue yonder. Every now and then I peeked over my left shoulder without turning my head enough to make it too obvious and realized in great disbelief that I was looking at the profile of my pilot, and said to myself, *Yes, that is Harry and this is you.* I pinched myself, took a deep breath, and prayed. We circled over my house, and I wanted to send a message to my family that I was in that low flying plane hovering over the house with none other than "geetar Harry." They would have been so surprised. Horrified may have been the more appropriate term. As the moments ticked by and I was beginning to feel rather safe, I decided to settle back and go for the ride.

All of a sudden, Harry announced our time was up and we were going to land. I panicked, because I didn't care for landings in the super jet liners. How was I going to handle this in a two-seater and with Harry at the helm? If I had actually thought about the landing, I wouldn't have been there. I kept saying to myself, *Elaine is the one who should be here, not me.* But as reality would have it, that wasn't what was going on. So I buried my head in my lap and prayed really hard, asking God to bring this piper in safely. And then, before I had chance to go into a state of full blown anxiety, Harry said, "You can sit up now." Yes, we were on the ground—a landing that left me ever so grateful to Harry. From that moment on, I knew it would be okay to oblige his second hand invitations. I might say when that little plane landed, it was like a feather on the runway. Thank you Lord. I will be in church every Sunday, no exceptions—especially to show my gratitude. Not only could Harry carry a tune, he could bring his piper in for a glorious landing.

---

## TYPICAL AMERICAN GIRL
### *by: Elaine*

Beauty pageants were not something I related to on a personal level. I would enjoy watching the Miss America Pageant, but that is where it stopped.

There was a time some years before I entered the Typical American Girl Contest, while at Girl Scout Camp, and was chosen Miss Camp Frances. It did not make sense to me what wearing bathing suits had to do with recognizing one's personal attributes. It was a fun-and-games kind of happening, and I somehow was less than enthusiastic about joining in the event. That reserved, serious side of me was dictating and truly became a winner when Carole agreed to accept the little trophy.

Here I was, five years later and seventeen, a junior in high school finding myself in a similar but up-scaled happening.

A bathing beauty I was not; however, my boyfriend had a different thought.

Back in 1958, one of the major New York newspapers had a contest in its Sunday magazine section called "The Typical American Girl."

After days of consideration, I agreed to have my boyfriend submit my photo and statistics. I was rather reticent about having my posed picture, in a bathing suit, posted in a publication that would reach thousands. Though, as I viewed the winner each week, it really didn't seem all that risqué. *And* I came to the conclusion that I would not move beyond a contestant.

While I never considered myself very competitive, I had come to realize that I would clearly delight in being a winner. This did not diminish my reticence about my major three measurements being in the newspaper. The fact that they made one's background and plans for the future important was a good buffer. After all, this contest was labeled "The Typical American Girl," sponsored by a key New York newspaper. My questioning mind contemplated the parameters as I often do.

Weeks after submission, an envelope arrived with the newspaper's return address. As I raced to open it, I could feel the conflict only slightly. Inside was a letter of congratulations with the expected date of publication for my submission to be displayed. Assuring the reality of the moment, included was a check. At that point, any reticence changed to pure pleasure.

Yes! Now what?

My overzealous boyfriend had not had the foresight to see the consequences of submitting the picture in the paper. Shortly thereafter, several letters arrived from cadets at the Naval Academy, and students at close-by colleges asking me to consider a date with them.

*by: Carole*

Seeing my sister's picture on the cover of the magazine section of the paper seemed surreal. I thought she looked so pretty and I felt she should be a winner, but did I expect to see that happen? Not really. Realizing the limited number of contestants to be selected for the cover shoot, only one a week for several weeks, seemed like a remote chance at best, but the judges did not agree, and there she was, a winner. Yea!

Here I was ready to capitalize on our twinship, something neither of us gave thought to. Here I had an instant perk awaiting me with no effort on my part. This was no time to denounce similarities.

One of the cadets from West Point Military Academy who wanted to take Elaine out on a date got a return letter telling him of her twin sister, me. And much to my excitement, he said that he would like to invite the twin to West Point for a weekend. My heart was beating with anticipation and some expectation of having a great time, which indeed it was. While it was not a love connection, it was a weekend to remember. The social graces of the cadets and the ambiance of the academy made for a beautiful memory.

Thank you, Elaine, for sharing your win with your twin!

# THE TYPICAL
# AMERICAN GIRL

**W**HEN THEY ASK Elaine Sloan, "Are there any more at home like you?" she might justifiably exclaim, "Why, yes, exactly like me – my twin sister." There are three daughters in the Sloan household in Darien, Conn., which is where this week's winner lives. Elaine, 17, is a senior at the Darien High School and is taking an academic course. After graduation, she plans to study dental hygiene. And, of course, she's thinking of marriage, too.

Outside of her own home, Elaine feels at home in the water (or on top of it, ice skating) or on the dance floor. Bust, 35; waist, 24; hips, 36, are the statistics. She stands 5 feet 8 inches tall and weighs 135 pounds.

## RULES . . .

Any girl 16 or over, single or married, is eligible to enter our Typical American Girl search. (Models, entertainers and previous weekly winners are barred.) Just mail us a recent color film of yourself, preferably in a bathing suit. Do NOT send paper color prints OR negatives from which color prints are made. We require color FILM, upon which are seen all the true colors photographed. Many a possible winner has crossed our desk unchosen because the lady was on print or negative. If still in doubt, ask your film dealer. This is important. Include in your letter your age, occupation, height in stockinged feet, weight, bust, hip and waist measurements. Tell us about your family, your hobbies, where you went to school, what you studied and your ambitions.

We will print a girl's foto each Sunday through June 28, 1959. Each weekly winner gets $25. At the end of June, 1959, when the search ends, all those weekly winners will be eligible for the grand prize of $500, second prize of $100 or third prize of $50. A full-page color-foto of the grand prize winner will be printed in this Magazine. Entries postmarked after midnight May 18, 1959, will not be eligible. Address entries to the Typical American Girl Editor, SUNDAY NEWS, 220 E. 42d St., New York 17, N. Y. Each letter must include a statement releasing the film for publication in the Coloroto Magazine. We will return unused pictures if you send us a stamped, self-addressed envelope.

Elaine, 1958

## KLENZIOD EQUIPMENT, HERE SHE COMES
*by: Elaine*

A unique question
A unique offer
A life changed

One day sitting in my office about six months into a new job, the president of my employer's parent company came into my office and said, "Sloan, you don't happen to know anyone just like yourself do you?"

My response, "Funny you ask, I have an identical twin sister."

He proceeded with, "I will be retiring soon, and my son will be taking over the business. I think it would be nice if he had an associate." He continued by asking if my sister was available and whether she'd be willing to make such a move.

Conversation ensued, and Carole was contacted to come to Pennsylvania to consider the option. She accepted the offer, came to Pennsylvania, and is still at the same place of employment.

This is one of those situations where I will tell you all things happen for a reason. The company I was with, Hydro Components, kept popping up in the help wanted ads. I was nearing the point of looking for work, but had not yet gotten serious about it. On occasion, I opened to the help wanted section of the local paper and barely scanned it. However, I was noticing that for consecutive evenings of looking, my eyes were drawn to one particular position and nothing else. The position was advertising for someone to manage an area of a water treatment company. My marketing and sales background did not seem to be a match, but something in the way the ad read caught my interest in a big way.

The ad instructed, "No phone calls, must send resume." Not having an updated resume and viewing this ad for the third time, I decided to do a chronological letter for consideration. Something was drawing me to it. Why could they not have a phone number? After creating a special letter, I looked in the paper to see where they wanted the resume sent and there was the same ad, only this time, a phone number was included. I called that very day and got an appointment for the next day.

After being interviewed by the president of each company, I was hired on the spot. I was excited! My prayers were answered. I wanted a change in employment and the manner in which this evolved told me it was meant to be.

As circumstances ensued, the question became, *Was this meant to be for me or for Carole*? I do believe sometimes we are a conduit for what happens to the other. In this instance, Carole got ongoing career employment and I shortly thereafter found myself looking for employment as the affiliate company closed its doors.

Just months later, Carole had also been hired by the parent company. She moved to Pennsylvania, and there we sat in adjoining offices. That was a first and kind of exciting. However, it was short-lived, for within a year of her taking that position, a division of the company I worked for was purchased by a California firm. As irony would have it, the president, who was the only one who would have moved, was diagnosed with cancer, and he did not survive long enough to make the transition. The other division of the company I was responsible for was phased out.

We had adjoining offices no more. It looked like Carole was meant to be in Pennsylvania.

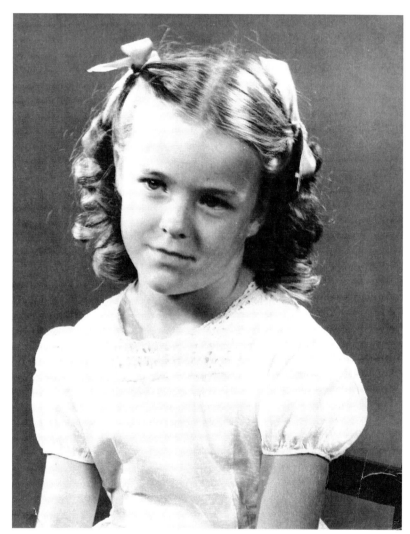

Elaine

Carole

Elaine

Carole

.

# Escapades

Growing up and not experiencing an escapade or two might leave one having missed out a little in life. We had a few before we were old enough to understand the dynamics of reacting, I believe, to the twin forces. (What one didn't think of, the other did.)

Then there were a few that came about due to life's circumstances, and in those cases, they were not thoughtless moves but our attempt to make things better.

———— ❧ ————

## DIAPER DOLLOP

It was a beautiful spring day in March and the twins were nestled in for their afternoon naps or so their Mother thought. They were lying there in their respective cribs looking at each other figuring out how to be creative.

Yes, creativity was something in which they excelled, maybe not so surprising with a father who was an inventor. They were always masterminding an event or so it seemed.

As they giggled back and forth not truly able to articulate their thoughts, they started to dance in their cribs, causing them to move across the uncarpeted floor toward each other. Now it was quite a lively dance step, and they found if they stomped with certain vigor, the cribs would inch along amazingly. It didn't matter who came upon this wonderful idea first; they were both in step in no time. The outcome may not have been decided at this point, but they were determined to connect, that is for sure. Now, as if dancing their cribs across the floor was not brilliant enough, they were on a roll, and stopping was not in sight.

They were finally able to grasp hands. Yea! They had arrived at their destination. Where this next idea came from, heaven only knows. It was with great enthusiasm they were about to try their first attempt at finger painting. Yes, as they gleefully took the contents of one diaper, they began their design on the bedroom wall. The rich brown color began to look like a dark and gloomy winter landscape when all of a sudden their glee was interrupted with a loud undeniable shriek. As they looked around, standing in the doorway, putting an abrupt end to their escapade, was Mommy Dear.

The story goes their mother did not know whether to laugh or cry before the great clean up. But this was for sure, before they knew what happened their cribs were returned from whence they cometh.

*—Carole*

## RAINING FRUIT

I remember an event that took place when we were all of four years old.

Mother was having a furnace problem and needed to call a repairman to see what was happening. She asked us to be good little girls and play with our toys while they descended to the basement. We were happy to oblige, at least for the moment.

It's not certain which one of us instigated the forthcoming event, but we were on the move, taking full advantage of being alone. We made our way to the dining room and hoisted ourselves up on the buffet by pulling chairs together and supporting each other on the climb up, making our way to the fruit bowl we so often would look at from afar. It was this beautiful, crystal-like bowl always brimming over with delicious fruit. We took our respective places, one on each side of the bowl and got started. We took a bite, just one bite, out of each piece of fruit. As we bit the forbidden fruit, we threw it on the floor in excitement, one piece after the other, until the bowl was empty.

Mother was down stairs hearing these pieces of fruit hitting the floor and wondering what on earth could be going on. Not wanting to leave the repairman downstairs unattended, but hearing this unfamiliar noise from above, she reluctantly made her way to see what her little darlings were doing. As she entered the room, one look told us the fruit was not the only thing that was going to be on the floor. She was visibly unhappy at the sight she encountered, but fought to keep her composure with the repairman below us. Mom would not want to lose it with him in the house. Yea, Mr. Repairman! She quietly but briskly removed us from our perch on the buffet. The ride to the floor was a lot quicker than the climb up.

She took us to the famous closet (this was the closet that housed all of our toys and where it was expected to be in some resemblance of order when playtime was over) and told us to find something to do. This closet was rather intimidating for two small beings. Fortunately, by the time the repairman left, we had redeemed ourselves by staying put in this great big closet—yes, big enough for us and our toys.

—*Carole*

# BILLY BOY STARLETS

"Billy Boy"

Oh, where have you been,
Billy Boy, Billy Boy?
Oh, where have you been,
Charming Billy?
I have been to seek a wife,
She's the joy of my life,
She's a young thing
And cannot leave her mother.

Did she ask you to come in,
Billy Boy, Billy Boy?
Did she ask you to come in,
Charming Billy?
Yes, she asked me to come in,
There's a dimple in her chin.
She's a young thing
And cannot leave her mother.

Can she make a cherry pie,
Billy Boy, Billy Boy?
Can she make a cherry pie,
Charming Billy?
She can make a cherry pie,
Quick as a cat can wink an eye,
She's a young thing
And cannot leave her mother.

How old is she,
Billy Boy, Billy Boy?
How old is she,

Charming Billy?
Three times six and four times seven,
Twenty-eight and eleven,
She's a young thing
And cannot leave her mother.

And the show begins.

Starlets Carole and Elaine descend the stairs and take their special place on the side of the living room to the right of the stairs. The far side of the living room was brimming with their parents and parents' friends.

Rehearsals were few to nonexistent, so here we were, having announced ourselves and studying each other quite closely to see who would start the song. You know how one looks at another with an intensity that speaks without words, but the message is clear?

*You first.* The problem is when the other looks back with the same message.

What seemed to last for hours was only seconds; the song began.

Elaine attempted to sing the questions in the song, and Carole belted back the answers. In either regard, there was little melody. It didn't stop us from proceeding with our enactment. Imagine the skit anyway you will, and we feel certain it would have an edge on our performance.

This might have been the impetus that caused my mom to give us singing lessons. Our singing teacher, after the second or third class, suggested that it might be a better investment to give us dancing lessons.

*—Elaine*

## THE KINDERGARTEN KLING

What should the first day in kindergarten look like? One would hope for a smooth, happy transition.

As we walked around to the side of the school, our footsteps got shorter and slower, with my mom trying subtly to hurry us along. By the time we reached the door entering the school, we were no longer holding her hand but had clutched onto her coat.

As we entered the building and headed down the stairs to our assigned room, Mom had us clinging to her coat, one on either side. At least we had her in proper balance as our cries of protest echoed in the vacant hallway outside our impending classroom.

As our new teacher appeared and peeled us away, leading us into the room, our octaves increased to the point we were ushered into the coat closet with anticipation of peace and or quiet ensuing. It did.

Once we were led to our desks, the school year began. In a very short time, we were looking forward to each school day.

Having each other didn't help the instant moment of separation, but once we realized we were in this together, perhaps there was some strength in numbers—a kind of unspoken phenomenon.

—*Elaine*

## JEWELS FIT FOR A PRINCESS

It was a typical school night in the late springtime. We had met our Dad at the station and walked home with him as we did in those days. That was our ritual and our special time with him when he was not traveling.

As we were walking into the house, my Dad noticed something under the car. We went to see what it was. It was a little box, and when we opened it, the prettiest pendant type necklace was revealed. It was gold in color with a real big sparkler in the center of many little ones. We were so excited; our eyes were fixed on the jewel. We thought it was for us, and we promptly went into a heated discussion of who would get to wear the lovely piece first. Mother assured us that no one was going to wear it, that it needed to be returned, because it was worth more than we could imagine at our young years. Surely one of our "little boy suitors" had left it there. Yes, secret admirers at such a tender age!

It seemed apparent that when we would be walking home from school, which we loved to do, the little boys would follow us and throw stones in our path. That made Mother not too happy, but we saw it as a display of affection. What kind of affection was not clear, but we asked her not to do anything rash. She reluctantly agreed to yield to our whimsical wishes. Now she was faced with yet another concern. To whom did the jewelry belong? We were faced with the fact that the gift was going back. Since Mother was not certain to whom it belonged, it was decided we would wait and see.

It was only a few days later when the doorbell rang, and upon answering it, there appeared yet another little box. In the distance, we saw the "gifters" running away. Yes, Sherlock Holmes would have been proud to solve this mystery so quickly. We told mother, and then showed her the pretty jewelry. She knew the only way to see that the jewels went to the hands of the respective mothers was to do it herself. Hence, Mother had the supreme honor of returning the gifts to the very surprised mothers who had not yet missed their gems. As you might expect, they were ever grateful.

—*Carole*

## MORE THAN APPLES IN A TREE

It was said that we had a little bit or maybe a whole lot of tomboy in us when we were young. We were about 10 years old, and to find us outside playing in the woods or climbing trees was not unexpected. It was second nature to us. Fostering this desire to be outside was natural since, in those days, there was no family TV—nothing to keep us in, and anyway how many times can you clean a room? Mother may not have agreed, but she was delighted for us not to be underfoot all the time, especially since there were two of us.

At this juncture, we were living in a house that was off the main road with this very long driveway, perhaps the length of a city block. Halfway between the road and the house was this magnificent apple tree. It was situated on a slight hill as the driveway made a bend, leading down to the house. It was a great tree and had so many sweeping branches and so many leaves and blossoms, not to mention its ideal location. In our exploration of nature, we decided this would be a perfect tree in which to create a little hideaway.

At certain times of the year, when it was in full bloom, *no one* would know we were there. This lonely beautiful apple tree became the object and the end of our search. We could even hide from our mother and father, or at least say we didn't hear them when they would call us to come home, thinking we were out in the woods. This gave us a little more time for a respectable response. How amazing to be so close and yet so far. Our visitors would slowly ride away as we witnessed the whole thing from above. Sometimes we felt bad about it, but the intrigue superseded the guilt and once the coast was clear we climbed down from our hideaway in the tree only to return again and again. We sat on high and watched the world go by, literally. This appealed to us for many reasons.

On Saturdays and sometimes after school, the boys would come to play. They rode their bikes down the long driveway and knocked on the door for us to come out, and Mom would always tell them we were out playing, so the story went. Our visitors would slowly ride away as we witnessed the whole thing from above. Sometimes we felt bad about it, but the intrigue superseded the guilt and once the coast was clear we climbed down from our hideaway in the tree only to return again and again. Looking back now, I am not certain why they didn't get tired of receiving that message. Once again, as mother would say, "Hope Springs Eternal."

Yes, we had made ourselves this wonderful little place way up in the apple tree where we watched the happenings of life around us. We thought we were in utopia. When we finally confessed to our mother about our hiding place in the tree, she *reluctantly* kept our secret. Not to mention the response time to her "come home" calls was shortened considerably. She liked that!

—*Carole*

## DANCING DAFFODILS

We would like to paint a picture for you. Imagine a quarter of an acre field with a lovely little cottage surrounded by a white picket fence. It is a magnificent spring day, and the crystal blue sky is the home for a few puffy white clouds gently moving as clouds do. In front of this cottage is a cherry tree in bloom and a field of yellow daffodils. It is like there is a rich yellow carpet laid out in front of this cottage. Every inch is covered with daffodils. Add a gentle springtime breeze, and there is a dance going on—a rhythm of nature taking place as these daffodils sway to and fro. There is a peace, a harmony in this painting.

Along come two sweet little girls who are swept into the painting. Yes, what they see is irresistible. All these beautiful flowers would make a gorgeous spring bouquet for their mother. Surely as they pondered the idea, the owner of the cottage would hardly miss a few flowers. As they got closer, they grew more and more excited at the thought. As they arrived at their destination, they paused for a very brief moment and decided the flowers would not be missed. It looked like the house was vacant.

Elaine and I laid our schoolbooks down, took one more look at each other for approval, and got underway. Oh yes, we were dancing in the field just like the flowers, picking a daffodil here and a daffodil there. In our excitement, we picked enough daffodils to open a small flower shop. We had all the flowers we could hold and still manage to pick up our books. With such delight and hearts full of love, already forgetting where the flowers came from, we headed for home to present to our mother her gift.

Our mother, was swept away by the beauty of the daffodils and the thought behind this gesture of love. When she got her composure and asked where the daffodils came from she was caught up for a moment in what to do. Having strong moral values she felt the flowers needed to be returned no matter how sweet the act.

Elaine and I looked at each other again, but not in glee this time. It was more like in apprehension of what lay ahead of us. As we walked back to the little cottage, we were contemplating who would be the one to deliver the message. And maybe, just maybe, we were right and no one lived there. As we rang the bell and waited anxiously, much to our chagrin, an older lady answered the door. Elaine, bless her heart, told our story, and the lady kindly but sternly said we could take the flowers back to Mother, but we were never to pick her flowers again.

A lesson was learned—never to assume.

Years later, Mother said she, in some regards, was sorry she made us return the daffodils.

—*Carole and Elaine*

I wandered lonely as a Cloud
That floats on high o'er Vales and Hills,
When all at once I saw a crowd
A host of dancing daffodils;

I gaz'd—and gaz'd—but little thought
What wealth the show to me had brought;

And then my heart with pleasure fills,
And dances with the Daffodils.

*William Wordsworth*

Poem was written by William Wordsworth in 1804 and published in 1807 in *Poems in Two Volumes: Moods of my Mind 7.*

———— ❧ ————

# MOGA NO MORE

Elaine and I were the only two non-Catholics at the Mother of God Academy. It was not a problem for us, but it was for our parents, who wanted to be active on the board and were denied the opportunity to be in an appointed position because we were non Catholic. At a PTA Meeting, you could have heard a pin drop when our father asked the question, "How is that possible when my daughters are permitted to be here as full time students and pay the same tuition?" This was undoubtedly a first and there was no answer forthcoming to ease his frustration. This did not make them too happy, but they succumbed to the dictate. Hence, we stayed enrolled.

The teachers were all nuns except one male professor who, while teaching us, sat there eating graham crackers and grapes. I remember this clearly because there were times we wished he would have offered us some. We loved grams and grapes!

There were only two others within the school who were not nuns. One, a school administrator who was an extremely large lady distinguishable by her silk dresses, always with a Chinese mandarin collar. And then there was her sister, who was slightly mentally challenged and walked around the school reporting anyone not in sync with the rules. She had an uncanny way of showing up just when you didn't want to see her.

Then there were the boys who had a liking for us. On a couple of occasions they showed up at the old Victorian mansion that housed MOGA. They would ring, ring, ring the bell, never once, always three times. This shrill little bell awakened the whole school. This did not go over in a big way. As Elaine and I sat in our classes and heard the bell ringing, we would hold our breath and count the rings praying it wasn't a secret admirer. It felt good to have secret admirers, but not at MOGA, a girls' academy. Sometimes they would stay there and ask to see us and other times they would run away before the door was answered.

Oh how we wanted to be back in public school. There seemed no way to make that happen.

Still indelible in my mind is that glorious day when we made the executive decision to walk straight to the administrator's office and turn our books in. *Wow...* what were we thinking? But we knew we had each other. We always had each other when it came to creative opportunities and out of the box choices. Oh, yes, we were shaking in our boots because following the major meeting with the administrator was the phone call home to share with our parents how brave we had just been. Of course, it wasn't going to be bravery from their point of view.

I remember our stepping into the administrator's ominous office, as she stood there bigger than life. As we moved forward into the room coming face to face, all of a sudden, we didn't feel so brave anymore. Actually if we could describe the feeling, it had turned into two undeniable cases of the jitters. There was no assessing what the other one was feeling, for we were already deep into the action. The speech we made was a blur and remains a blur, but we remember laying our books on her desk and maintaining our composure so as not to run out of the office. Feeling so proud of ourselves, we went skipping out of the school. The big moment had come. I remember fumbling for the change to make the call home arguing as to which one of us would give the breaking news. We kept reminding ourselves that the courage came in our longing to go back to public school, which was not our parents' desire. Education for their children was important to them and at this juncture, they thought MOGA was it.

More than anything, I remember the unceasing silence on the other end of the phone when we delivered the breaking news. We gingerly asked, "Mother, are you there?" There was no response, so we bid our goodbyes and headed for the bus. It was a very *long* ride home that day. We were glad Mom was home to receive our "Call of Bravery," knowing it would surely buffer our appearance. Fortunately, we worked it out and went back to public school.

—*Carole*

## FLEEING TO TEXAS

We were nineteen and not terribly sophisticated when Carole and I left our home in Connecticut, headed for Texas—Dallas, to be exact.

It was soon after high school graduation that we decided we needed to spread our wings. My mother had a bridge partner whose two sons were headed back to school at Texas A & M.

You might say we hitched a ride with careful consideration. Our home life at that point was unfortunately a little too tumultuous, thus our decision. We were actually teaming up for the first time during our teen years, forging forward with high hopes.

Off we went, without a clue as to what we would find upon arriving in an area of the country hundreds of miles from where we had ever been thus far in our lives.

We arrived in Dallas early afternoon, and after discovering there were no vacancies at the YWCA, we scanned the local newspaper and found a room to rent rather quickly as our friends needed to drop us off and move on to campus. It never occurred to us that we wouldn't find a room—a rather grandiose notion, one might say.

On a quaint residential street was a lovely little home, owned by a Mrs. Zacharius who ushered us to a bedroom and bath she had for rent. She softly voiced a four word instruction, *no food in room*. We took the room immediately and followed the rules but not to the "T," the exception being food. We filled the bottom dresser drawer with apples, rolls, and tuna, hoping the aromas would not waft into her hall. We really liked her and felt fortunate, but we did not have the means to be eating out. In our naïve way, we thought her biblical name would work in our favor. Oh, youth!

Other than the actual job hunt, our most immediate goal was what to wear for the search. So we went to one of the local department stores and started our shopping spree for corporate dress. Our ideals were definitely loftier than working in a store; after all, we had taken the academic course in high school. Surely, there was something of special interest awaiting us.

So here we were in Dallas headed out to find the job that would allow us to stay in the deep southwest.

What we did was against everything we had done to that point, of nineteen years. We wish we had a photograph to share; perhaps you can conjure up an image. We settled on gray wool flannel straight skirts, modestly below the knee—mid-calf actually, white generously ruffled blouses, gray and black sleeveless fitted vests that paired with the skirts and black high-heeled shoes with a strap across the top.

It was an outfit that made a statement—no two statements. Needless to say, every job we applied for that day bore the response that if one of us got homesick the employer would lose two, not one employee. Somehow, we didn't get the message to stop knocking on doors side by side.

The nature of what we had on made us feel more identical than even being identical feels.

We were not only going door to door together, but also looking like "two peas in a pod." It never occurred to us the actual image we were projecting to these impending employers. No one was brave or adventuresome enough to give us a chance despite our verbal reassurances.

I must admit, we did discuss going solo door to door; but it didn't happen. Where was all that independence we had worked so hard for over the years? However, we convinced ourselves there was power in numbers.

A major financial decline was looking rather imminent.

Within a couple weeks and after some major conversation, I was on my way back to Connecticut to stay with a friend. Carole wanted to stay longer and lived with Harry's girlfriend who was an airline stewardess. (Remember Harry with the geetar?)

Within another couple weeks, Carole was on her way back to Connecticut, too.

*—Elaine*

Dad and Mother

Carole and Elaine—13 days old

Mother and "the girls"
Carole and Elaine

Carole and Elaine

Carole, Dawn and Elaine -Staged by Elaine

Plaid coat sets made by Dad and Mother
(We don't know who is who)

Carole and Elaine

Carole and Elaine

"The girls" at Pear Tree Point
Carole and Elaine

Carole and daughter Dawn, Navy
Elaine and son Richard, Army

Elaine and Carole

Elaine and Carole

Elaine and Carole

Elaine and Carole

Elaine and Carole

Elaine and Carole

Carole and Elaine

Elaine and Carole refurbishing antique bootblack stand

Carole and Elaine—Blowing out birthday candles

Carole, Mom, Dawn, and Elaine

# Mother's Happy 95th Birthday

Carole, Mom, Elaine
At Mom's favorite William Penn Restaurant

Mother, Carole, Dawn and Elaine

Elaine and sons
Richard and Stephen

Carole and daughters
Dawn, Susan, and Cher

Elaine and grands
Derek and Brandon

Carole and grands
Ashley, Michael, Zachary, Mario, Samantha, and Josh

# Comparative Chapters
# on Shared Events

We have taken significant events as they relate to segments of time. They are written from each of our perspectives. It has interested us to see how differently we perceived the same event. Neither of us saw what the other one wrote until our work was finished; no changes were made to the content.

One might wonder how our perceptions could be so different. As previously suggested, it captured us with wonder as well. These times clearly paint a picture of how life is no more than a perception of the perceiver. How very interesting to contemplate this possibility.

Could it be that our findings in the style that we have incorporated within this chapter might rock the previous gold standard for qualifying eye witnesses? Here are twins: same gene factor, mirror image, raised in the same environment, with strikingly different perceptions of the same happenings. Take two eyewitnesses of the same event testifying in court; which is correct? One might think this could create a possible turning point in the legal field.

# MAPLE AVENUE YEARS
## *by: Elaine*

As we approached the corners of Main Street and Maple Avenue in Metuchen, we were heading to our new home. This is my first memory at three years of age. My twin, Carole, our sister Dawn and I were getting off a bus just across the street from our new home. Mom had gone on ahead to take care of a few things before we arrived.

My father was on one of his lengthy business trips. Just weeks before leaving, he moved the family into a home that was not acceptable to my mother. He had found the home rather quickly the night before he headed out on yet another trip. He had promised my mother that certain things would prevail—a good school for Dawn, a safe neighborhood for all of us, and perhaps another criterion or two. After trying to make it work for a number of weeks, my mother felt we needed to make a change and found a rental in Metuchen a number of miles away. Again, my mom was taking the necessary lead.

As we departed the bus and walked across Main Street onto Maple Avenue, as new as everything was, I was comfortable with my sister Dawn leading the way. Her reassuring and positive style prevailed. I couldn't have labeled her leadership style back then, but I was delighted she was Carole's and my sister.

What about Maple Avenue? We were moving into a large house, sort of like a two-story colonial with a third floor/finished attic, enclosed sun room off the living room that had a fire place, French doors separating the living and dining rooms, and an enclosed porch leading to the backyard—lots of potential play area and lots of special memories to ensue.

The kitchen was large with a dining table and benches in an alcove that looked so cozy; however, Carole and I had each other so we shared a small table and chair set to consume our meals. I remember protesting on occasion and being reassured that we would not be at the little table if we did not have our sister as a dining companion. It was not unlike what one would have for her dolls' playhouse, except this was the real deal. I do remember, joining others at the dining room table on occasion as we grew older. I was extremely happy when we outgrew our special dining set.

There was more to our kitchen; a large closet that housed Carole's and my toys. Every now and then we would be relegated to cleaning the closet, which would seem to take forever. It often became the quick catchall at the end of the day when all our toys had to be put away before retiring.

The kitchen brings to mind a scary happening. My mom was baking and we were playing nearby when she opened the oven door. There was an explosion and flames shot out of the oven. She called out telling us to go roll on the dining room rug and keep rolling. We rolled and giggled, rolled and giggled, not realizing for a moment what had happened, wondering why we were less than supine on the floor. Flames bursting from the oven singed my mother's eyebrows and hairline. All and all we were fortunate there were no serious injuries or damage.

One afternoon as we arrived home from school, mom asked us to go into the sunroom in a slightly irritated tone. What had one of us forgotten to do? Other than that I could not think of a reason for her being disenchanted with either of us. As I entered the room peeking around the corner to assess the situation before rushing in, I caught sight of shopping bags and clothing arranged on the wicker sofa at the far end of the room. Could this be for Carole and me? We were being treated to some wonderful new things: skirts, blouses, dresses and more. Excitement reigned high!

While we were not dressed alike, we usually had like clothing in different colors. We would take turns getting to choose the color we wanted. I remember never liking pink. And to this day, I do not enjoy pink in clothing.

What female doesn't like new clothing? I think age is immaterial. Finances were limited when Carole and I were growing up. By the age of fourteen, we made a lot of our own clothing. If I asked for a new dress or outfit, the response would be, "I'll buy you the material and you can make it." This day was such a treat, for while what we had was nice, the quantity was limited.

Memories on Maple Avenue did not stop here.

There was a large tree-laden lot next to our house on the far side of the garage where we spent many hours in the fall, with neighborhood friends of varying ages, creating leaf lined houses and school rooms for play. If you can envision looking at a blue print and looking down at this lot from above that is what you would see. We loved designing these elaborate layouts and then playing school or whatever was determined by our design. Of course, this was a seasonal activity—one highly anticipated by all. All we needed were fallen leaves, rakes and imagination.

Metuchen brought our first ventures away from home like visiting friends on the block. Best of all was when we were old enough to walk over to my sister, Dawn's and brother-in-law, Art's new apartment She seemed so grown up and beautiful to me ~ well, she was. I wanted to be just like her.

One doesn't have to walk forever to get somewhere… walking would no longer be our only way of reaching a destination. Carole and I were introduced to our new first two-wheel bikes—English bikes with the brakes on the handlebars. We never had tricycles that I can remember. You might say we were starting out big. Actually our feet could not touch the ground, but they could reach the blocks on the pedals. My father was the one to send us forth with a wing, a push and maybe a prayer. I'm not certain how we managed not to fall, but he was there to stop us as we came back to the starting line. After a bit of practice he turned it over to us; we were becoming pros or so we thought.

One day as we toured around on our bikes we ventured down Linden Avenue. I say down, because there was a steep hill leading to a stop sign. As Carole went to stop her brakes grabbed and she went flying over her handlebars and on to the heavily cindered road. I rushed to help her. The next hours were in a doctor's office having cinders removed from her knee. I almost felt like it was my knee that was injured. Empathy was at play.

Did you ever dream of being someone special? I have always wanted to be a singer; could it be because I cannot sing—AND there is proof. My mother used to go around the house singing; she could not sing either, but probably thought it would be wonderful if Carole and I could. So at a very early age, we were sent for singing lessons. As we entered this well-kept older house, I remember a highly perfumed fragrance that permeated the air. As the instructor led us to her piano area, I observed she was a very heavy set woman with what I remember thinking looked like bullfrog eyes. Children can be so unkind, but it was the best description I could come up with. In later years I came to realize she probably had a thyroid problem and I felt concerned for her even though it was many years later when I became enlightened. After just a couple classes of having us sing scales, she suggested to my mother that it would be a better investment for her money if she gave Carole and me dancing lessons. So on to ballet we went for the shortest period. Dancing didn't seem to be our forte either, at least not ballet.

Then came trips to New York as we ventured into the field of modeling. We were just finishing our portfolio at John Robert Powers', when my mother took a trip to Texas. We had only gotten to modeling children's clothes in the Sear Roebuck Catalogue.

Mother was not well when she returned from Texas and therefore we had made our last trip to New York. The modeling agency called a couple of times to see if we could come back, but alas our lives took another path.

While still on Maple Ave, Carole and I had our first overnight trip away from home, to an aunt's house in the farming section of New Jersey. The drive was about two hours from our home on Maple Avenue. We were trying to muster up our courage to be away from our mother overnight; being very fond of our aunt it seemed like a good idea. However, we were going into a new and very different environment which included an outhouse and pie made from condensed milk. It was pumpkin! The condensed milk was the offender. Those are the two things I remember most. To appreciate the latter statement, we basically never had desserts while growing up. I know it must be hard to believe that those two factors could make a difference, but that is what I remember being the deal breaker. Two hours after my mother left my poor aunt was listening to our whimpers and realized she would be lucky if we made it through one night. We did and my mom came back for us the next day. We were missing what we knew our creature comforts to be. Even though we were young we had learned our manners well enough not to be specific as to our discontent.

Then there were birthday parties… the first one I remember was on Maple Ave. Actually that was the last of our birthday parties until our adult years. I am a great proponent of celebrating birthdays. It's celebrating the existence of a special someone. Sharing a birthday party with Carole meant twice the fun. When living in the same area we still celebrate together, otherwise we celebrate each other from afar.

Maple Avenue brought another vivid memory—not so pleasant. We had a garbage truck driver who appeared to be a rather large man with piercing eyes. Often when we were out playing the truck would come along and stop while it was being loaded with trash. The driver would stare at us in a way that was very unsettling. It seemed like he sat up real high in his truck and was intently looking down. At that age I just knew he scared me. We would stop what we were doing and run inside when we saw the truck coming. Every Christmas Eve, as long as we lived on Maple Avenue, I would have this scary dream that we would be playing in our driveway and the garbage truck would come along and the driver would start to get out of his truck. The thought was that he would kidnap us and we would race through our yard to the house. We were always safe, but not without a scary race for safety. Once we moved away those dreams stopped.

One last glimpse of Maple Ave… in our spacious well groomed yard we had a perfectly shaped Dutch Maple tree that caught my attention every time I looked at it. I didn't know why, I just knew it did. There was a lovely dogwood as well; however, there was something extra unique about that maple.

If I have paper and pencil in hand I am likely to start doodling; trees are one of my favorite doodles. How fitting that I came to love maple trees on Maple Avenue.

*by: Carole*

Maple Avenue brings back so many sweet and warm memories compared to some other places I have lived.

We were only about 3 to 4 years old, but I remember clearly the comfort of my older sister as we rode the bus to look at this possible place to live. Mom never had Dawn do much with us, because she did not feel it was her responsibility to care for the twins. In Mom's decision, I believed we missed out on a lifelong nurturing of a relationship. Fortunately, we have made up for it over the years, but we missed out on experiences young people normally have. I don't believe Mother ever saw this.

Our home was a modified colonial on a pretty property with the most beautiful dogwood trees I have ever seen perhaps since then as well. When the dogwood was in bloom, it touched my heart somehow. I am almost certain my love of the fall came from living in Metuchen. This home had such a wonderful lawn. In the fall, the trees would shed their leaves, and Elaine and I would become mini architects. We would actually design fun floor plans out of the leaves creating what we thought to be exquisite homes. Heaven only knows how we felt when a strong wind would come along and blow the walls of our home down. Fortunately, that did not happen too often... but we saw it as one of the hazards. Yes, our leaf houses were designed right down to the bedrooms, bathrooms, and closets. You know it had a toy closet big enough for two kids to fit in! I always wished my older sister Dawn could have played architect, too.

There was something about the front steps, a backdrop for birthday party pictures at our Metuchen home. It was also a place to congregate when friends would come by to visit.

I loved being outdoors on Maple Avenue, but then I am an outside kind of girl. I have always preferred being in nature. I remember under the side porch, this little family of skunks had made a home for themselves. They were there actually for a while. We just let them be. This made me very happy. Every now and then, the little family would come out for a walk and return back home. It was really sweet. Then one day, they went away. Looking back, I was glad they went on their own accord. I wasn't certain how long the welcome would last.

In the house, there was a bright and beautiful sunroom. We had a little bunny that lived there in its cage. I can't recall the bunny's name, and I am not certain that he was with us for any real length of time. We also had a sweet little cat affectionately called Arthur Bootsy named after my sister Dawn's boyfriend— the Arthur part, that is! The Bootsy part was an elementary whim.

One day, Mother summoned Elaine and me into the sunroom, and to our glee, there were all these beautiful clothes. What a surprise it was, because when she called us in, it sounded rather serious, and I remember walking rather timidly to meet with her. When Mom bought us clothes, they were alike in style 90 percent of the time, but different in color. Elaine and I danced in delight, selecting which colors we wanted and excited to have these beautiful things. (As strange as it may seem, when I dressed my little girls, who were each five years apart, often I would buy the same color and style. Can you figure that?) The greatest gift my mother and father gave us was to raise us to be individuals. They never focused on our being twins to my recollection. Our family did not have much money when we were growing up; we were what I would have called a family of limited means, so this was an exceptional treat. Mom had a gift for acting and making it look like she had something even when she didn't.

There was a time in our lives when Mother thought singing lessons would be nice for her girls. She always wished she could sing, and I believe it was fulfilling her dream. The singing teacher's home was a short walk from our house. As she opened the door, there stood this fat lady, big enough to fill the doorway. Forgive me, but that is what my young mind was thinking. She had eyes that looked like they were popping out of her face. I found this somewhat alarming, but Mother explained later that it was a health condition. Once we got past the introductions, Elaine and I were ushered into her parlor. A baby grand piano took up most of the room. She sat down at the piano, struck a note, and demonstrated the scales that she wanted Elaine and me to try. I felt very uncomfortable. I didn't know what Elaine was feeling, but I thought it had to be similar to my feelings. Now at the end of the scales, she picked a song "One Alone." Do you know that song? Two little girls singing "One Alone" created quite an amusing moment. Well, long story short, it wasn't long before she said to Mom, "If I were you, I would get them dancing lessons." What a perfect way to squelch any desire to sing ever again.

Elaine and I often walked to meet Daddy at the station when he would come home from work. It was several blocks away. We lived in a safe community, so Mom was okay with it as long as we promised to stay together. Daddy would always arrive with a treat in his pocket for us. We would have to pick which pocket, but the treat was always the same—Chuckles, but we loved playing the game anyway. It was so much fun to decide which color we would eat first. It was more about time with Daddy than the candy, because he wasn't around very much. He traveled a lot. At that time, I thought he was the smartest, most handsome man in the world. His travels left Mother to take care of the important things, and I know my sister Dawn was an enormous help to her.

Our time on Maple Avenue may have been the beginning of my dislike for traditional medicine and the acceptance of a holistic approach on a subconscious level. In my early years, I came down with a very serious ear infection. I remember the doctor coming to our home almost every other day for a long time to administer a penicillin shot to cure the infection; an alternative approach would not have been a consideration. As it turned out, it was one of those times that the antibiotic was the chosen treatment. Once again, the doctor made his unwelcomed appearance, at least from my point of view, and stuck my little arm with this great big loaded needle. Ouch! Well on the last day, he and my mother chased me all around the house, because I had decided that I would not succumb to one more shot and wondered why this was happening to me and not my sister. Thank goodness for a large house; it kept them at bay a little while longer. Much to my chagrin, they did catch me, and one last time that long, long needle pricked my tender skin. I cried! I have often wondered if all this penicillin is the reason that I am allergic to it today.

While living on Maple Avenue, I received my first new bicycle. It was an English bike, the kind with brakes on the handlebars. This called for great coordination, or so it seemed. One day, I went a little too far on a street that I do not believe was on our given and approved road map. Actually, in this little neighborhood, all our friends were only a block or two away, and walking to and from was always fun. Now, I was on my bike, and had peddled into an uncharted area. I started down this rather steep hill feeling free as a bird, when all of a sudden, I realized I was at the crossroad. I pulled on the brakes, the front brake had much more force, and to my surprise, I went flying over the front of the bike, ending in a rather abrupt stop on a cinder-laden road. Elaine came to the rescue. She ran for help. To this day, I have the scar where the doctor plucked out cinders one by one for several days; it was very painful. What a test of my endurance. Mom did not need to chastise me; life had done a great job. So much for not staying on course!

There was the garbage man who would wave hello from his big, red truck. He would come down the street, and I would get this eerie feeling, because when he looked out from his window way up high in the truck, it felt like he was looking at you with x-ray eyes. I am not certain I would have described it that way then, but that was the feeling it elicited in me. I came to find out that Elaine felt unnerved by him also. I wondered why that was so. I told my sister that several years after moving from there, I had dreams about the garbage man, and she said, "Funny, I did, too!"

It was a wonderful little community. Walking in nature and riding bikes was an invitation always waiting, and Mother felt safe to give us leeway. Yes, I have warm memories of Metuchen.

# ISLAND HEIGHTS
*by: Elaine*

Years later, I went back to visit Island Heights, the special little town on the Toms River in New Jersey where we went every summer as children.

It was amazing how small everything looked: the homes, the shopping areas, the boardwalk that outlined the waterway, the pavilion that was a part of the beach area, the yacht club, in view of the beach—that always held a mystique. Years before, all of this seemed so grand.

Nonetheless, despite my illusions of grandeur, some of our summers were quite awesome.

My mother's sister-in-law, Lillian, was a favorite of my mother. She was one of my favorites, too. She had a lilt to her voice and a smile that made me want to smile with her.

Aunt Lillian owned a year-round home in Island Heights about four blocks up the hill and four blocks over from the beach we frequented—the place where we spent most of our summers. It was so easy to share conversation with Aunt Lillian. She was a good listener and responder.

At one point, we rented a summer cottage right beyond a hotel just across the street from the public beach. What made that cottage so special was not the fact that it was only a half-block from the beach, but that right next door was Siddons with hand-dipped ice cream. Back then, an ice cream cone was heaven's delight. It would often be an end-of-the-day, right-before-bed treat, and on a hot summer night, it didn't get better than that— not at four, five, or six years of age, anyway.

Swimming lessons started for Carole and me at three years of age, compliments of the Red Cross. Since our summers were spent at the shore, by the bay, or at the ocean, there was no question in my mother's mind that her daughters should know how to swim—particularly since she herself felt deficient in the skill.

On one side of the beach was a two-level pavilion. From the center of the pavilion was a pier that extended probably about thirty feet long with a "T" shape at the end. I remember venturing out on the pier, careful not to get too close to the edge, until the big day came when my swimming was proficient enough that I could jump or dive off the very end, usually on the "T" side that faced the beach. That seemed a little less risky. The other "T" side faced a boat basin, and if you looked across the water from that side, you would see the yacht club.

Oh yes, the yacht club, the Island Heights Yacht Club—I loved the double swinging doors that led into this building of mystique. Why do I say mystique? Well, you had to be a member to go inside, and as a young child, I was very curious. I wanted to be a member so I could go inside and see what everyone else was seeing and experiencing.

I would often stand on the boardwalk and watch the hustle and bustle as the members walked in and out of the club, most often heading toward their boats attached to the dock that had the same "T" shape as the pavilion down the boardwalk where membership was not required.

Our sister Dawn had Yacht Club privileges. Somehow, I liked that thought. It was almost like being a part of something without being, kind of a vicarious connection.

Recollections abound as to Island Heights and Seaside Heights.

My Aunt Lillian and her four sons, our cousins—Ernie, Joe, Lynn, and Tommy. Two were closer in age to Dawn, while the other two were closer to Carole's and my age. We looked forward to our adventures each summer. Dawn, Ernie, and Joe spent their summers at the yacht club and sailing while Lynn, Tommy, Carole, and I aspired to time on the pavilion at the beach or trips to the ocean. It was almost like having brothers for the summer.

Daily excursions to the beach to go swimming and playing on the pavillion were highly anticipated as we ran in bare feet on the summer's scorching hot pavement to get there. Crossing the streets caused you to pause for just a moment and wonder why you hadn't put shoes on. Nevertheless, next time, we still were without shoes.

There was a pond with fish swimming freely around gracing our Aunt Lillian's front yard. I would often pause to watch the fish and query as to how this lovely little haven came to be. I sensed peace while watching fish swim without a care in the world. I wanted to swim like those fish in the water with a carefree spirit.

Lightning strikes every now and then. Within my Aunt's home was a living room with an archway that you would walk through into a hall where the bedrooms were. When we would have an afternoon thunderstorm, I remember having to sit in the living room and be still. On two different occasions, as we were sitting there waiting out the storm, lightning struck right inside the house at the base of the archway and traveled up one side across the top of the arch and down the other side. That was an "I don't believe my eyes" moment.

I remember the gorgeous sunsets. If you imagine a town where half of the peripheral is a partial circle edged with a boardwalk, areas of beach, an occasional pier that extended into the often-calm, smooth as glass water, sprinkled with a sail boat here and there, and a rosy sunset on the horizon, it could be Island Heights. The wonders of nature were clearly in focus.

The ocean called to us as well, Seaside Heights. That was a family outing, as it required going by car. There were two bridges we had to cross to arrive at the ocean. Crossing those bridges was rather unsettling. They were made of wooden slats and you could hear the tires of the car cross each one, or so it seemed. There was always a sense of relief when you arrived at the other side. On one trip across, there was a fire on the bridge that was quickly extinguished, thank heavens.

Seaside Heights was the amusement park area at the ocean. What a treat that was! I used to enjoy watching all the activity as much as being a part of it—maybe more. This was where I developed a fear of Ferris wheels. There was a large Ferris wheel at the end of one pier, so that when you were revolving around, you were overlooking the ocean. When at the top, it felt like you were literally over the ocean. On one venture circling around the great heights, Carole and I were in a car that stopped at the top due to a mechanical problem; a problem that lasted far too long for my sensitive spirit. Carole, much braver than I at that moment decided it would be fun to swing the car we were in; rocking it back and forth as fast and as high as she could. As I begged for mercy we seemed to go faster and faster, higher and higher. I knew when I touched the ground that would be my last Ferris wheel ride... at least with my sister.

I guess all young ladies like to recall a summer romance. I had a summer romance, which consisted of one movie date and one good night kiss, along with hours of meeting and talking at the pavilion. Then the summer ended and we said goodbye, two years in a row.

What I can add to the memories of those summers in Island Heights is that it was wonderful having a sister to share those adventures.

I have gone back to Island Heights twice since those early years and have been amazed at how small and close together everything seems. It's not surprising but perhaps slightly disappointing that the magnitude of those moments is slightly diminished.

Carole and Elaine in Island Heights

---
*by: Carole*
---

Water, water, water, take me to the water. This was and is my mantra. I am certain in the earlier years I didn't know it to be a mantra. It may have seemed like nagging to my parents. Even though we were not raised in a family of comfortable means, when I look back, I am surprised at what we did have and what I would call the good fortune to experience.

Yes, we spent our summers in a little rented home on the opposite corner of the street from the town dock called "the pavilion" in Island Heights, New Jersey. Down the street, not many yards away, was the town yacht club for members only. I remember times watching people come and go through the swinging screen doors and wished I could slip in behind them to see what was on the other side. It seemed like a big, exclusive secret lay in there. It would be one day several years later that my older cousins, who were sailors, would present the opportunity to solve this mystery. I finally got to see what was on the other side of that screen door that had captivated my attention for so long. I was surprised, even as a young child, at the very modest parlor and meeting places for the elite boaters. Yes, this was my sense of it. After that visit, my fancy was no longer victim to the illusion. It was just another door. However, I was always excited to see my cousins, because they were so nice, and they were sailors who had stories to tell of their experience in the Bermuda and other international races. While I knew very little about the boating world, I did know this was very special.

Island Heights was also where my Aunt Lillian lived. I loved my Aunt Lillian, she was one of the nicest people I knew, and visiting her was like a special holiday. My mother always said that, too. We would go to her home in the evenings, sit around this big dining room table, and play hearts. Hearts was a card game that seemed to draw much attention. I could never understand the game, but it gave us the opportunity to see one of my older cousins who may be dropping by.

Tommy, my younger cousin, who I thought was so adorable, lived there, and Elaine and I would play with him often. Aunt Lillian's home had this neat upstairs. It kind of seemed like a hideaway from the rest of the house. There was this center staircase, and it went up to a big room that the stairs divided. Its design created a good spot for playing hide-and-seek from one side to the other. It was lots of fun.

In the front yard of my Aunt's home, there was this little fishpond and I loved watching the fish. It was a lot different from seeing them in a fish bowl. I loved it out there. Across the street, there was this little old lady named Dr. Steckler. She always said it was best to eat bananas when they were turning dark and had brown speckles on them. I didn't like bananas then, and I don't like them now. Maybe there is some truth to what she said, but I am not sure.

The pavilion at the beach was the town meeting place, or so it seemed. Extending from the pavilion, across the street, was a dock that went out into the water forever. It was long, like a narrow runway. I would feel very brave walking out to the end, surrounded by the water that was way over my head. Walking back would seem to take even more courage, but these feelings never kept me from venturing out to the end. Initially, I would timidly walk out on the dock, because my swimming skills were not so advanced, although mother did see that we had a lesson or two. As time went on, I welcomed a new sense of bravery. Need I add that having my sister with me holding my hand from time to time was just a dose of courage added to the mix? The pavilion also had a top floor and it was so wonderful to go up there and feel the summer breeze and see the shore from a grander view.

Another highlight of that summer living was to experience Siddons. Siddons was another meeting place. It was one of the town's ice cream parlors, just up the street from the town dock. When walking in it felt so exciting to see the ceiling fans spinning and the bar stools lined along the counter laden with all kinds of goodies. Temptation was knocking. With great anticipation, we would take our place at the counter and debate in our tender minds which delicious goodie to experience that given day. I can still remember the smell of the homemade strawberry ice cream. At times, it seemed to permeate the senses—yum to memories of Siddons and directly across the street was another one of the town's ice cream parlors, Vierick's Ice Cream, where all the delicious flavors were homemade. This called out to many, but I loved the ambiance of Siddons better and seeing the kids that hung out there. Anyway, Siddons had swinging screen doors!

There was my cousin, Lynn, and his girlfriend, Barbara, I recall vividly thinking they were the most beautiful, loving couple I had ever seen. I wondered if I would have such a relationship one day. They married and raised three wonderful boys. It was fifty some years later that I ran into them at our cousin's, their brother's, funeral. It's funny in life how it sometimes takes funerals and weddings to bring families together. This meeting turned out to be a very good thing. It has been special to rekindle that relationship, which was in the earlier days only an admiration from afar. Today we gratefully have nurtured a forever friendship.

Another special thing about Island Heights was the short ride to the ocean. Now we didn't do it all the time, but when we did, it was memorable and exciting. It was on the other side of the bay. There was this very long bridge about a mile and a half or two to the ocean side. The bridge was very old and wooden and only had one lane in each direction. I clearly remember listening to the sound of the wheels of the car as they made their way over the planks. In the middle, there was a drawbridge for the boats to go through to the other side. To my young mind it was awesome sitting there waiting for this mystery to happen. I vividly remember this one particular day we were gleefully journeying to the ocean at Seaside Park. As we approached the center of the bridge, all of a sudden the traffic came to a halt and the cars started turning around one by one to retreat back to land. This was quite a feat. There was a fire on the bridge. I didn't know enough to fully panic at that age, and my parents seemed to be maintaining their composure. I remember the excitement that it caused and felt some apprehension as to how we would get back from whence we had come. Fortunately, there were no accidents, just disappointed families not to be by the ocean that day, and this did somehow seem to override the gratitude for safety.

At the ocean, there were all kinds of exciting happenings. A few of my favorites were the low tide and the amusements at Seaside Heights. Low tide to most would not be such fun, for it would be lots of walking to the deeper waters, but on certain days— not all days—the ocean would cause little pools of water to form in the sand, and I loved them. As you were walking, you would fall into these pockets of water. Sometimes you would see them and sometimes you would not. Also at low tide, you could find the prettiest seashells. I loved the ones that had a subtle pink or a pearly grey in them. While I collected many seashells, I don't remember doing anything special with them, but I was always excited to give them away.

My other favorite thing at the ocean was the amusements on the boardwalk. It was so much fun. The ride in particular that called to me was the Ferris wheel. The reason I loved it so much was because it was perched on the end of the dock, and when the Ferris wheel cars would come down from the tippy top, you would have this illusion of going right into the ocean. I used to love swinging that little car back and forth, back and forth, and Elaine would keep saying, "Stop that, Carole." But sometimes I didn't hear her, because I knew our rides were limited and wanted as much of that feeling as I could get.

At the time of this writing October 29, 2012, we were experiencing Hurricane Sandy—ever to be known as the "Perfect Storm"; and I saw on television that the Ferris wheel at Seaside Heights had been dumped into the ocean—my heart sank for a moment remembering all those precious memories.

I believe my early days by the sea were the beginning of my great passion for this immense body of water commonly called the ocean. I always felt carefree and a sense of real freedom to be there. The smell of the salty air called to me, as the breezes would gently blow through my hair (a feeling I adored and still adore). Another great feeling was the waves splashing playfully over my feet as I walked along the beach. Building sand castles with Elaine, making them beautiful, and dreaming as if they were real was a favorite, too. I loved and still love it all. I would feel such abandon when by the seashore.

Life in Island Heights was, without a doubt, an experience in my young life that will forever be with me. The memories are indelible in my mind.

---

## A COUNTRY INTERLUDE
### by: Elaine

I was definitely raised in a matriarchal family with no question that my strengths as a female were derived from my mother. As a small child, I admired her abilities and wherewithal and felt safe. We were a family of females with my mom, Frances, twin sister, Carole, and sister, Dawn. Having a sister ten years older was almost like having another mother, though she was not authoritative with us, she was very capable, sensitive, and caring, like a bright star with a gentle touch. As to the four of us, I would say, we girls had it together. Our family pattern did not fit the "WASP" middle-class norm, which in that period of time, the 40s through the 60s, would have been that of a patriarchal family.

My father, Stephen, called Dick by most, came in and out of the picture during those early years as he traveled in his work endeavors, often being gone for what seemed like months at a time. He was a mechanical/combustion engineer and inventor for a small New York firm. As a young child, recollections of my father were sparse; my most outstanding vision was of him walking home from the train station when he was in town. Carole and I would watch anxiously for him coming down the street; at the first point of recognition, we would start running to meet him, not sure if we were actually racing to see who could reach him first, for the outcome would be identical. As we approached my father, we called him "Daddy," he would reach into his pocket and bring out two packages of Chuckles—one for each of us. They were such fun to eat as we contemplated which enticing color/flavor we would have from first to finish. It was kind of like a game as we devoured the five pieces. Double contemplation certainly made it more fun. Had I been alone with my Chuckles, the merriment would have paled.

On one of his many trips, I almost want to say infamous trips, he took my mother with him—Texas being the destination. I remember my parents in a serious debate; my mother wanted to take Carole and me, and my father suggested that we stay on the farm where he grew up, with my grandfather and Aunt Margaret who was living there so my grandfather would not be alone. She was a nurse who had turned my grandfather's living room, then referred to as the front room, into a nursing home area for two bed-ridden male patients. There was a curtain between that room and the kitchen.

My father, in his desire to win the debate, made the promise that Carole and I would spend each weekend at my aunt Hannah's home a number of miles away. My mother, who had issues with Margaret, was most fond of Hannah, and that was more than likely the drawing card that allowed her to acquiesce to my father's desire to leave her girls at home. My father had won the battle.

So my mom went away with great reluctance, but with reassurance from my father that we would be fine. Why did my father not want us to join them? I can only think that it was a business trip, and he and my mom would be freer to move around without two young daughters trailing along. Dawn was in college at the time and therefore was fortunately not uprooted during this period.

This was a critical happening in our lives, for our mother as we knew her never returned. She came back a troubled soul. We later came to realize our mother had had a nervous breakdown. As a third grader, having to adjust to a very different school situation and home environment, a harsh aunt, and a list of unpleasant happenings that went on and on, being topped by missing my mother and older sister, was not easy and was probably a time in my life when I was delighted to be a "twinie." It was certainly the one period when I was not fighting for individuality.

I liked that Carole and I had each other. The long walk along the somewhat desolate country road to the almost one-room schoolhouse was not a trek that culminated into a happy destination. There were a number of grades in our classroom and that is about all I remember except for bringing our lunch, which I was unable to eat most of the time as my Aunt Margaret insisted on putting clumps of cold butter on the bread, which gagged me. A request for change was to no avail, for how dare I challenge the preparations of a nurse.

On one of our walks home from school, a strange man pulled up and offered Carole and me a ride to our grandmother's house, saying he had been asked to pick us up. Well, of course, we knew my grandmother was not living; therefore, in less than seconds we had taken off through the fields of high grass. Even though my grandfather's house and the school were on the same road, they were about a mile apart with only one or two farm homes in between. We ran and ran, not stopping until we reached our destination and grateful the questionable stranger just drove off. As we told our story huffing and puffing, we were simply reminded never to take a ride from a stranger. Could it have been that the desire to reach our momentary home was so great that living there looked better? I have no answer for that question.

If we didn't iron our clothes to my Aunt Margaret's liking, she would tell us we could not go over to Aunt Hannah's. On several occasions, you might say our aunts duked it out, for Aunt Han, as we called her, knew our situation, and had promised to pick us up each Friday and keep us until Sunday. She was a saving grace. Carole and I loved our weekends with Aunt Han who lived in a home that had a restaurant attached. She was such a good cook, and my Uncle Tank would let us have birch beer with dinner. *And* we got to spend some time with our two cousins, Gail and Sandy. Sandy was closer to our age; however, there was enough difference in age, I am certain we thought it was a greater treat than they did. My Aunt Han was most like my father of all his sisters. I thought she was so wise. To this day, I remember her telling me never to go to bed angry. Not being one to harbor anger does not make that difficult, but I thoroughly understand the merit of that statement.

Back at the farm house, those drawn curtains, I mentioned, that separated the kitchen from the living room, were a bit of a mystery even though I knew there were two ill gentlemen on the other side. I do remember one day getting a glimpse when my Aunt Margaret was feeding one of the patient's tapioca pudding. He was alarmingly thin which I noticed as he sat on the edge of his bed trying to take in that chosen nourishment. I couldn't help but wonder if he disliked the tapioca pudding like I disliked the butter. There was something in that scene that, as a young child, concerned me tremendously; was he going to be okay? Not a question I was going to ask out loud. He was still there when we left to go back to our real home on Maple Avenue. It was years before I could eat tapioca pudding.

Most disturbing on our stay at the farm was my Aunt Margaret not letting me talk to our mom when she called, saying that it would make us too homesick. I was crushed. The phone would ring, and our mom would be right there, just inches away on the other end of a phone, and I couldn't get to her. How I wanted to hear her voice. The tears welled followed by a sleepless night mulling over and over again my longing to just hear my mom's voice. How could my aunt be so unfair for I promised not to cry if I could just say "hi". On one such occasion, days later Carole and I received a wonderful package and I remember thinking that mom was telling us this was another way to reach us. There were blue gingham dresses, cowboy boots and belts (a touch of Texas) and white gloves. I believe there were other items, but that's what stands out—oh, a little strand of pearls.

You might be wondering about my grandfather; I did, too! He was present without being all that present. I believe I heard that he drank a bit, but I just remember him sitting in the basement on a straight-back kitchen type chair and sleeping.

After a very long six to eight weeks, I looked up and saw my mother walk into the country school classroom where I was sitting. She looked so good to me, I could not contain myself and stay seated, I just could not wait to hug her; the feeling was mutual. As glorious as that moment was, little did I know that my world, the one that changed just eight weeks earlier would never be the same, nor would my mom.

My mom was different. She looked the same, maybe better, for I missed her so much; but her spirit was broken. She had become a fearful and phobic person, not wanting to go out, unable to cross bridges, and unable to handle many of her normal responsibilities. At times, it would be difficult for her simply to function through the day, and different friends would come in to be with her and us. My life had become a pattern of emotional survival.

It was never clear what happened on that Texas trip that tipped the scales.

I can say here, had my mother not portrayed strength in my early years, I would not have weathered those about to ensue nearly so well.

Farmhouse—Vineland, NJ

---
### by: Carole

My father always traveled when we were young, and that seemed the norm. It felt like he was never coming back at times, because his trips were so extended, but he always did. My mother was there with a caring heart carrying on and trying to maintain a loving home for her children as best she could.

There was a time when my father, whom I called "Daddy," was to go on a business trip to Texas and was asking my mother to go with him. This was not the norm and may have been the first time that he had asked her to join him. I remember some conversation about Elaine and me going, but it turned out differently, and we were delivered to our Aunt Margaret in the rural countryside of New Jersey. My Mom was not happy about this and I came to understand why even at my young age.

Aunt Margaret was my father's sister and lived in the farmhouse where they grew up, down deep in hillbilly country, or so it felt to me. My familiarity was with urban living. I knew I liked urban better than country, and I still do. My grandfather lived there with her and I believe he was my saving grace on those long lonely days. He was a very kind and quiet man and would play with us, which filled my lonely heart. I missed my mother so much and Daddy not so much. I was accustomed to him not being present, but not my Mother. She was the strength that held the family together.

Staying on the farm with Aunt Margaret for several months seemed like several years and was bitter sweet. I remember three highlights: one was Grandfather, one was Aunt Hannah and the other was the one-room schoolhouse.

I remember one time when Grandfather was sleeping in his rocker, which he did after a day's work, Elaine, and I gleefully adorned his balding head with curlers the best we could. Looking back, he was such a good sport. I am sure he was awake the whole time. While we didn't play beauty salon with Grandfather all the time, he was still there and he softened the long hours.

The second highlight was spending delightful weekends with Aunt Han. She would pick us up on Friday afternoon; we loved her appearances. On an occasional Thursday she would pick us up to go to the Catholic Stations of the Cross service. I looked forward to spending time with her and my cousins Sandy and Gail. Aunt Han was so very kind and caring, and she knew how important our visits were. On those times when Aunt Margaret did not want to let us go Aunt Han would do whatever was possible to change the course of events. Aunt Han would take us shopping and buy us some very pretty clothes. She was always trying to make the visits sweeter than our week.

Then there was the walk to the one-room schoolhouse. It was a long and unsettling at times, with only a house or two along the way, however, it provided a great escape from being with Aunt Margaret. But, I had my sister, and there were times when we held hands ever so tightly until we arrived at our destination. I would not have wanted to walk alone.

One incident stands out clearly in my mind. As we were walking along one day, a small truck pulled up alongside us. The driver asked if we wanted to ride to our Auntie's house. As our hands found each other's, our grip told the other of our fear. We said a resounding "NO." We had been taught not to talk to or take rides from strangers. Once we started running the truck pulled away. We watched it in the distance go right on by Auntie's.

Upon our arrival, we related the story to Aunt Margaret, and she had no idea who it might have been. We liked the walk less after that experience.

Yes, it was a long several months, and there were phone calls. Once in a while, Aunt Margaret would decide we shouldn't talk with our parents, because it made us sadder. A couple of times, a box arrived with treats. I remember a western belt that was so pretty and western boots. That only slightly took the edge off, and only for a moment. Those treats were like treasures to me, because they were from Mother and Daddy.

Then they returned, and joy filled the air for a very brief time—something was wrong. It wasn't long before we felt our Mother never returned. She was there in person, but that was all. She was so different. What happened to her in Texas, I wish I knew. What I do know is that it caused her to have a nervous breakdown. I missed her in a whole new way.

---

# MANSFIELD AVENUE YEARS
## *by: Elaine*

We left Maple Avenue due to my father being transferred from Peabody Engineering's New York City office to head the Research and Development Department in Stamford, Connecticut.

This new venture brought us to Mansfield Avenue, and what a shock! My folks had rented an old carriage house down a long, curved driveway nestled in the woods. Did I say old? I did, and I was not exaggerating. This antiquated carriage house had wood siding that looked gray, because the shingles were so weathered. Wow! It needed painting. I questioned whether it ever had the first coat of paint except for the red trim around the windows.

At first, the idea of a "carriage house" sounded kind of unique and special. As children, we picked up on the nuances that were expressed in conversation. As if the thought of a "carriage house" took it steps above what it really was. I loved the potential that imagination could add to a situation.

So here we were driving down this long driveway and looking at our new old home on Mansfield Avenue. The fantasy "carriage house" was not reality. There was no turning back. This was certainly not a match from where we moved.

As we reluctantly entered the front door, reassuring ourselves that our parents had not rented sight unseen, Carole and I hurried up to the second floor to see the bedroom we would be sharing. That seemed more important than anything else. It was a large room that could easily hold two full beds and accompanying furniture. There was a slight variant from what otherwise seemed a normal room; if I put a marble on the side where I entered, it would find its way downhill to the other side of the room. I knew this because we couldn't resist the temptation to confirm our observation with the first round object we could put our hands on. It worked!

The garage attached to the right-side of the house was rather rickety and so was the large storage room at the end of the porch that ran along the back of the house.

In my youthful assessment, I was delighted that this "carriage house" backed up to a track of woods and had a large pond in what looked to be our back yard. These factors brought about what would become favorite activities of mine: hiking, climbing and skating. I wanted skating lessons so badly, but it was not in the budget, so I self-taught.

Oh, I wanted piano lessons, too. My father thought we needed a new piano, which was not in the budget either, while my mother thought any piano would do as long as it was in tune. I agreed with my mother, but a piano was not forthcoming.

This aging carriage house, which my parents found located in an upper-middle class area of Darien, Connecticut, gave Carole and me the opportunity to be in a good school system. That was important to my parents.

Darien, for those who are not familiar with that area of Connecticut, was ritzy, upper class, and snobby. There were very few kids from the other side of the tracks. In fact, I am not certain there was another side of the tracks except for our carriage house. However, for some reason, it didn't matter, for Carole and I were welcomed into the fold of Darien just as if we were living in grand style. We had friends within the different cliques. I am not certain as to how that happened except to say that we saw everyone alike. My mother always said you could be friends with everyone. I had learned rather quickly one of the very first questions a young person was asked when moving into Darien. "What does your father do?" That bothered me, and I would find myself feeling that life is not fair. There were many times to come in my life where I would say life was not fair but nonetheless, it is what you make of it.

Off to the side of our long driveway was a wonderful apple tree. I discovered I loved climbing trees and would often venture to the top to look at my world from a different view. It was a perfect place to hide and still be at home. Hide, you ask? Yes, from whatever.

This was the home where I had my first crush, with a young boy in the neighborhood, who was two years older than me. At that point, two years older, seemed huge except for the fact that our mothers were very good friends. That little crush never went beyond a first kiss while standing outside in a freezing snowstorm and a refusal to let him drive me to a movie. There was no way my parents would approve of my riding in a car with a young driver.

Every morning before school, weather permitting, our pond was frozen solid. I would be out skating for about an hour, trying so hard to be a fancy skater. I wanted to do all the figure eights, twirls, back crosses, and jumps that I had seen others do. Lack of success was not from lack of trying.

Many years later, I took skating lessons on a work lunch hour. It took one lesson to show me how to balance my body on skates, and all of a sudden, I was doing so much of what I stumbled over in those early years. One little facet was the key: balancing. It was late coming, but still kind of exciting.

I remember one morning zooming out on the pond to spin around when all of a sudden I realized the ice was moving like waves under my feet. Oh my gosh, what was happening? I later learned that is what is known as rubber ice. To my good fortune at that moment Carole appeared; she liked to skate in the mornings as well. I was frozen with fear, afraid to move, until Carole found a board and stretched it out in my direction. It was still a distance from me, but I knew I had to move and better not wait too long. I raced to the board, stepped on it, and continued moving to the side of the pond. On solid ground at last and most grateful to my sister.

This old house had another ancient feature; a dugout for a basement. It was my father's desire to dig out a large area and create a somewhat respectable basement. It was a gargantuan task for untrained workers like my dad, Dawn, Carole, and me. But we plodded away at it—spoonful by spoonful, bagful by bagful. I guess my dad used a shovel!

It was on Mansfield Avenue that we had our first puppy pet. Our upfront neighbors, the Alfords—we referred to them as Aunt Bebe and Uncle Don—had a wonderful golden retriever, "Punch." Carole and I really liked him and wanted a dog. Thus, Pepper graced our lives. Pepper was a mutt, but a cute, mid-sized, and loved mutt—all black except for his four white paws, vest, goatee, and the very tip of his donut-shaped tail. He almost looked like we had dressed him up.

Pepper had a favorite hunting ground, which was through the woods to a private estate that bred Beagles. It took him a long time to find this fertile ground, but once he did, there was no keeping him away. As much as we tried to keep Pepper at home, every now and then the phone would ring and a disgruntled far-away neighbor would beg, "Please, come get your dog." It wasn't long before Pepper disappeared.

From Mansfield Avenue, we moved to Pleasant Place, Fairfield Avenue, and then Bonnybrook Road—all had their special nuances.

As I matured, I became very aware of the fact that life is what you make of it, no matter where you are. I wish I had realized the dynamics, back then, though I am not certain anything would have been different.

Old Carriage House

*by: Carole*

At nine years old, we were moving again. The only difference this time was that our sister Dawn was not coming with us. She was starting college, and she would remain in New Jersey where she was going to school at Douglass College, the women's branch of Rutgers University. This was going to be bitter sweet, because I would miss her very much. The blessing was when Dawn came home, Elaine and I shared our bedroom with her. I am not certain how she liked that arrangement, but I know I did. Having her close was always a comfort and still is to this very day.

We were a family of very modest means, moving into the exclusive little town of Darien, Connecticut. Perhaps you have heard of the book *Gentlemen's Agreement* written about Darien. Our first move was to this little old carriage house that sat far off the road with lovely homes lined in front on Mansfield Avenue.

While it was somewhat residential, I remember the excitement because there were woods all around in the back, a pond, and a stream. It was all so pretty to me.

I always felt so alive, even when I was young, being outside and that is always where I wanted and still want to be. Looking back, this little old carriage house became our home for several years. The first feeling when I walked in was the slant to the floors. You could have put a marble on one side and it would have rolled merrily to the other side of the room. That was okay for a little while, but Daddy decided it needed to be fixed. As he was no longer traveling with the company like he did for years, he set out to put a foundation under the old house. He calculated from his brilliant engineering mind, that a foundation would take care of the problem. Mother wanted to assist Daddy in doing this project, so when Elaine and I would come home from school, we were told to get a soup spoon and a brown paper bag. Can you imagine what this might have been for? We were two unhappy campers as we headed for the dugout. Yes, that is what was under the house. A dugout that was spooky and filled with all kinds of bugs. Our job was to dig dirt, yes with those little soup spoons and put it in the shopping bags. We slowly worked our way day by day into the dugout fearing the bugs all around us. One day, we were greeted with a joyous surprise. Daddy decided that we were not a help after all. Every time he would go to move the brown paper bags filled with the earth, they would break. Yea! Our task of being little miners ended marked with screams of delight. We were moving on up to bigger and better things to do with our personal time in the after school hours and Saturdays.

I loved the wintertime back in the woods, because down this steep incline behind our house was a sweet little pond. When it froze, it was the perfect place to skate. Elaine and I would often get up early and run down to the pond to skate before going to school. Again, this made me feel so alive. Our skating skills improved quickly with this pond in our back yard. It was perfect and beautiful. Before we knew it, we were spinning and leaping into the air and doing wonderful tricks on the ice. It felt glorious. In the winter, we would ice skate, and in the summer, go up the street to Rip Van Winkle's Bowling/Roller Skating club to roller skate. I don't remember Elaine going with me very often. I had come to love roller-skating, too, but it wasn't a favorite of hers.

On the way to the pond, there was this tree that had fallen over, and was draped artistically across the stream that ran into the pond. Now I say artistically because this tree had a dip in it that went from being horizontal to almost vertical before becoming horizontal again. I hope you get the picture. One of my favorite things to do was to run down this tree without falling into the stream. Then, one day, I didn't make it to the other side. Yes, I fell and all I can remember is hitting my elbow on a boulder near the stream. The pain took my breath away as you might imagine, and I decided it was time to give up this activity. However, I could not imagine anything taking my passion for nature away; it felt as natural as breathing. I was aware of all that nature had to offer me on that property surrounding the old carriage house.

One thing that stands out in my mind in particular was having this frisky little dog named Pepper. There was a dog kennel for breeding on the other side of the woods, and when the dogs were in heat, guess where Pepper was? Yes, right there in the middle of the dog kennel stirring up what he hoped to be a good time for himself. My mother would call her friend who had a little older son who would make his way through the woods and return with Pepper tucked under his arm only to open the back door and, anything but gingerly, deliver him back home.

We had a rather nice and good-sized hooked rug in the kitchen that Pepper slept on, and for some reason on this particular day, his rug had remained right there by the door. My sister and I were primping for a school dance, so fortunately her hair was in rollers. As Elaine leaned across the electric stove to put the spices back on the rack above the stove, her blouse rested on the burner where mother had not long before removed something she was cooking. Yes, my sister's blouse ignited, and she was in flames. All I could hear was my sister screaming and my mother hollering, "Don't run!" as Elaine was trying frantically to make her way out the door. Mom had the perfect sense to pick up Pepper's bed, the rug, catch Elaine to throw it around her, and happily was able to put out the fire. Elaine lay up stairs several days in shock suffering third degree burns, but fortunately, she did not have to be hospitalized. I was so happy to have her there with me. I wanted to keep an eye on her myself.

My sister and I used to walk downtown to the Sugar Bowl, a sweet shop, where our friends would meet. They had the best ice creams sodas and hamburgers. I missed going there for those weeks that Elaine was getting better, but we made up for it when she could finally go, and our friends were delighted to have our appearance once again.

I believe this is the one place growing up that I felt a sense of family. Our neighbors, who became Aunt BeBe and Uncle Don, played a part in that picture. Mom and Dad use to play bridge with them and that led to dinners and yard games together. We played croquet and tossed beer cans into cinderblocks stacked at different heights. That may have been the only time in my life I remember my parents actively doing something with us.

Yes, Mansfield Avenue is a place I will always remembe: the sense of adventure, the sense of family, and the portrait of nature that called to me.

———— ❊ ————

## PEAR TREE POINT SUMMERS
*by: Elaine*

One can hardly talk about living in New England and not mention the Long Island Sound.

There was always great anticipation as we drove across the little bridge and turned right following the road along an inlet stretch of the Good Wives River headed for Pear Tree Point. I was always curious as to how Pear Tree Point got its name without a pear tree in sight. There was a point, a long row of rocks, that became completely visible at low tide. They stretched from the beach about forty feet straight out creating a bathing beach area on one side, a boating and smaller bathing beach area on the other side. I remember loving to walk out to the very tip of the point, balancing myself from rock to rock; there was a challenge attached, and I liked that.

Names given to people and things always seemed important and interesting to me. I still would like to have seen a couple of pear trees. Names mattered then, and names matter now, which you will get glimpses of throughout this reading venture.

Pear Tree Point was for local residents and required a pass to enter the gate. For a nominal fee, that gate led to a beach and bathhouse—oh yes, and a concession stand. Darien was the home of many well-to-do families who did not frequent Pear Tree Point, as there were a number of lovely country clubs along the shore that seemed remote and kind of magical to me. In my early years, I used to think, if I could just see them to know the real differences, as I heard some of my friends talk about going to the "club." Nevertheless, I was happy being at Pear Tree Point for each time we drove in it was like, yes a repast for the spirit.

I never understood why, but basking in the sun was my time: my time to feel the relaxation from the heat my body was soaking in, my time to kick back and contemplate my life somewhat uninterrupted and my time to add a healthy hue to my skin. There were times when that seemed to me as good as it could get. Actually, it still has a great ring.

Time does change things and scientific research has now made us keenly aware of the risks of too many UV rays, but in those earlier days we had mastered the art of tanning; rolling from front to back and side to side at strategically timed intervals, considering cloud time in the process. Like a rotisserie, the process continued until something or someone that was more important came along—like a boyfriend. If another girlfriend had come along, she would have hooked her towel onto the row and gotten into the roll. There was usually a line four to seven towels long at any given time.

Even though Carole and I were encouraged to have our own friends and attended different events without the other, somehow I don't remember any visits to Pear Tree Point without my sister, at least not until many years later when I traveled back just to see how things had changed.

Pear Tree Point was no more than five miles from where we lived at any time.

My first encounter with Pear Tree Point was my mother's insistence on Carole and me taking Junior Lifeguard Lessons. We were slightly young for the class, but we were already good swimmers. Formerly our family had a summer home in Island Heights, New Jersey. My mom felt if we were going to be near the water it was a given that we needed to know how to swim. So by three years of age, Carole and I were stroking away in the water like fish in their total comfort zone.

Pear Tree Point had two large square floats about thirty feet from shore. At low tide, these floats that were about fifty feet apart were only inches deep in water, but at high tide, they became the destination of many divers. Carole was an exquisite diver and I trailed somewhere behind. I wanted to know why I couldn't get the extraordinary lift she had as she raised her body up from the float and came down into the water with perfect form without the slightest ripple in the water. Shouldn't we be able to do things identically if we wanted to? *And* when it came to diving, I wanted to. However, I never mastered that degree of perfection.

In fact, on one particular Pear Tree Point day, I decided to try a sailor dive. Have you heard of one? I had not before that day, but once I was told about it, I decided to give it a try. A sailor dive is performed by diving head first with arms down at your side—*not* a very good idea. But there were occasions despite being slightly shy, when I was adventuresome. This particular day, I was not shy. The outcome was not too pleasant as the water was not at high tide, and I headed straight for the bottom of the sound—Long Island Sound that is. As I hit bottom headfirst, I was fortunate only to have suffered some major scrapes and cuts and a mouth full of sand.

Heading straight to the nurse station, I kept telling myself what a risk I had taken and knew that would be my last sailor dive. The nurse treated my wounds and told me not to go back in the water that day, as I needed some healing time. Guess what? I not only didn't go back in the water that day, but I have not done any diving since that day. I feel certain if I had gone right back in the water and kept diving I would not have developed the fear that became ever so present. There have been times over the years when I have been fractions away from taking the leap;

now I just find my own graceful way for descending into the swimming mode.

We had a family picnic at Pear Tree Point, which was far from the norm. My mother, my father, Carole, and I one evening, after my dad arrived home from work, headed for Pear Tree Point! Since it was Carole's and my home away from home, we were so delighted for the opportunity to show our parents the extent of our water skills—swimming, diving, and a few water acrobatics. There were times when we were precocious enough to think we could mimic Esther Williams.

We hoped for high tide, for at low tide, the floats would appear adrift and you would have to walk so far out that by the time you could perform you were out of sight. We got to perform.

I will never forget Pear Tree Point and will always welcome the opportunity to go back to view our little haven on the water.

## by: Carole

I don't know if being born a Pisces has anything to do with it, but this I do know: my passion for the water is innate. It brings solace to my soul and always did, but as a young child, I may not have expressed it in the same way. I felt like a fish in water, as if I were in my natural habitat when I would be by and in the water. The ocean is what fervently calls to me, now, for I see it as a simile—the greatest expression nature offers of life, as the vast ocean represents the wholeness of life and each wave expresses individually as it caresses the shore only to return to know it's self again and again. How exquisite.

Pear Tree Point Beach was a place to lose myself in an environment I loved. I loved swimming and taking lifeguard lessons with Elaine at the beach. Mom thought it was important that everyone know how to swim, and I believe that was so paramount to her because of her fear of the water. She was not going to have her children grow up not knowing how to enjoy the beach and to be safe. I am grateful to her for that. My greatest love at Pear Tree Point was entering in the annual diving contest. I thought diving was a moment of freedom as you fly through the air. At least that is what it felt like to me. The swan dive was my favorite and gave me a sense of abandon. I think I may have won second or third place once or twice.

Also, there was waterskiing. I do believe I was born to be on water skis, for I truly never fell once—no, not even once! That was true for the slalom ski, which was my favorite, as well. Do you know what a slalom ski is? It is a single ski with one and a half feet grips in tandem, and calls for a greater sense of balance then you might expect. Again, I was truly blessed by my great love for the water and my agility in the water. The cream on top was my boyfriend whose family had a powerboat and a sailboat. We spent hours on the Long Island Sound enjoying my passion and theirs.

New England beaches are very rocky and when it was low tide, I remember walking for what seemed like forever on those rocks until all of a sudden your feet gratefully welcomed the softness of the sand. This was the only part of my Pear Tree experience that was not the sweetest of memories. In spite of this, I loved low tide and walking slowly and deliberately to deeper waters to take a swim, which felt so good.

There was an octagonal gazebo that sat alongside the concession stand and was on the pathway to a jetty of rocks that led out into the water. We use to love to walk out on the rocks and listen to the water lapping up against them. It is a sound I can still hear—just another beautiful sound of nature.

As the years went by, it was still the beach of choice, and I would frequent Pear Tree Point if only for a ride to appreciate the memories.

There was one period later in my life when I was working for a doctor who was only three minutes from this beach. We had a two-hour lunch break each day, so I headed for Pear Tree Point. I saw this as a gift. It didn't matter what time of year. I would park my car, bring out my favorite book, and sit there drinking up the sunshine and eating Snickers candy bars. I was a chocolate junkie all the way. When I took my car to the local car wash, they would attest to this. The attendants were always amazed at the number of Snickers wrappers they would pull from under the front seat when vacuuming the interior. It was with gratitude that I savored daily three things I adored—the beach, Snickers, and a favorite book—all the while making a living.

Yes, Pear Tree Point will always have a place in my heart.

# Comparative Chapters on Non-Shared Events

There were many events in our lives that Carole and I did not share, but they still speak to our similarities and our differences.

We have taken segments from our lives that allow you to get an idea of just how similar and yet different identical twins can be. You will see how there were times when these experiences intertwined despite our individuality.

## SCHOOL YEARS
### *by: Elaine*

My first school experience was like that of many, being separated from my mother to attend kindergarten. While I had a slightly independent nature, it was a separation nonetheless—one I had no control over and one I was not particularly happy about at that moment in my life. I can't tell you for sure whether having Carole there with me made a difference.

Franklin School in Metuchen, New Jersey went from kindergarten through twelfth grade. I thought it was kind of neat that Dawn was in the same school, though we never saw her during the course of the day. The building was three stories high and the older students were on the upper floors.

On occasion, I remember taking a note from my teacher to another teacher on an upper floor and feeling slightly intimidated by the larger students passing in the halls—intimidated and privileged all at the same time. Here I was being asked to make a delivery. However, the sense of trepidation won out. This feeling came about after one of the students in my class actually bit our teacher, causing her to take a leave of absence. She didn't come back for many months. As much as I liked Suzy—we played together often—I was in dismay. I realized my world was not so predictable. Our teacher did not come back the rest of that school year. Interestingly, this was in the second grade, and our teacher later became Dawn's sister-in-law.

When Carole and I were in the third grade, my parents started looking for a home in Darien, Connecticut. My father wanted to live in one of New York's bedroom communities, knowing that at some juncture his position would be relocated to Stamford, Connecticut.

This brought about a transition to Darien, Connecticut, and the Royal Elementary School. Carole and I were separated for the first time within a school system in fourth grade. This particular school system did not believe in having twins in the same class.

We were not only placed in different fourth grade classes, we were also adjusting to a new community and school system, plus being separated from each other for the first time. The school administration felt it would be prudent to have us repeat the fourth grade. This way we would surely function at the top of our class. As the years progressed, my mother often said she felt she had made a mistake in that decision, as we were bored long before graduation.

From my vantage point, even though Carole and I were new to an area, we were still busy creating our own lives and friendships. While our paths and interests crossed, we did some things together. Our striving for individualism was moving forward with certainty.

Looking back, it was interesting that there were about eight sets of twins in the Darien school system within a three-year grade range. I would often take notice of how they related and found myself evaluating their play on twin-ship.

Royal School brought another interesting facet into my world. My new fourth grade teacher was my first male teacher, a very kind man; but I was overwhelmed by his size. He was very tall and large. While I was happy he was my teacher, I did realize I felt slightly intimidated around very large men. This lessened as the years progressed. By the way, my father was not a large man.

For sixth grade, we went to the Royal School Annex, a wonderful old building on the Post Road. I am not certain what the building had been used for, but it had: wonderful dark woods, heavy trim woodwork, large windows, and shiny floors. I have one major memory while in this sixth grade class. One of the male students pulled a chair out from under a friend of mine who ended up falling on the floor. Most everyone thought it was so funny. Unfortunately, she injured her spine, was out of school for a period of time, and was unable to sit in regular school chairs for the rest of the year with her walking being challenged as well. This left quite an impression. To this day, I am perplexed at the humor found in one having an accident that can cause serious injury.

My next step was seventh, eighth, and ninth grades at Darien Junior High. Three things stand out in my mind during those years. When I walked into my new homeroom on my very first day, who was there but Carole. We looked at each other and kind of shrugged our shoulders. Not more than one class period passed when we found ourselves in the principal's office being asked which one was the "practical joker." Being serious students, we proceeded to express our surprise at being placed in the same homeroom. It was later found to be a mistake that was made by whoever did that area of planning for the new incoming students.

In the ninth grade, Carole and I went to a private Catholic school and, before the year was over, came back to Darien Junior High to finish out the school year. I had always been good in math, but had a little difficulty with algebra due to the changing of schools. At a PTA meeting when my parents were talking with the algebra teacher, they mentioned that I was interested in studying medicine. The teacher proceeded to tell them he would encourage me in another direction because I was having trouble with his subject, which was a very necessary area to master if you wanted to be in medicine. When my parents shared this teacher's sentiments, I was unfortunately discouraged and allowed it to deter my direction. I hadn't matured quite enough to trust my own inklings.

Another highlight at Darien Junior High was at a student concert when my boyfriend, who had a very excellent bass voice, sang "Some Enchanted Evening" and told me it was meant for me. Oh, young love, and oh, how I longed for a good singing voice. The only time I ever played hooky from a class was when I knew I would be requested to sing a solo, which I was not willing to do after one such episode, which brought about just too much laughter. I was sure not to let that happen again.

The Mother of God Academy (Ukrainian Order) came about because my parents thought it might be good for Carole and me to go to this private school in an adjoining community so as not to be a part of the distractions they felt came within a public school setting. We were okay with that. Out came our sewing machines, and we made uniforms to meet the dress code requirements. They were navy blue skirts, blazers, and white blouses. This was the first we had been together in the school setting since the fourth grade. Academically, I can't remember any benefits or lack thereof. Being taught by nuns was a new experience and certainly seemed to create a more serious environment within the classroom.

Less than a full year at Mother of God nearly came to a halt when my father was elected for an office within the PTA and was told he could not accept since he was not Catholic. Actually, I believe, Carole and I were two of only three non-Catholic students in the school.

I remember the older students wearing make-up to school and taking it off at the gate and putting it back on as they left headed for public transportation home. For the ninth grade, it had not yet become that important.

At Darien High, Carole and I found ourselves once again in separate classes. However, at this point, Carole and I were together for an extra-curricular activity. There was a small group of girls that wanted to start a drum majorette group for our football team. We had to convince our assigned teacher that we were very serious about twirling and supporting the team and were not about the "leg show" she suggested. I remember we were all rather annoyed by this particular teacher's suggestion and complained to the administration and reassured them of our forthright intention until we were given the go ahead.

My folks moved when Carole and I were in our senior year. Our house sold more quickly than expected and we had to move into an apartment in Stamford, a nearby town, until another home was purchased. The Darien school system agreed for Carole and me to commute to their high school and graduate from the school system we had been in since fourth grade, except for the three quarter year diversion at the Mother of God Academy.

Despite the kind offer, I made the decision to transfer to Stamford High and Carole decided to stay at Darien. When I look at that decision, I am not certain what motivated me the most, my stretch for independence or my discontent with other things. Even though we went our own ways, there was at time a level of competition that appeared in the relationship because of societal expectations.

As I am writing, I am keenly aware, more so than at the time, that this was Carole's and my first true separation in school. Not only were we not in the same classroom, but also in a different school and different town.

What was interesting was that Stamford was Darien's arch-rival in sports, particularly football. What had I done? Sitting in chemistry class my first day at Stamford High, the teacher made audible note that I had transferred from Darien High, and he noticed that I was repeating chemistry. Having gotten a C in Darien and my credits being nearly completed the decision was made to retake Chemistry. I did not like having a C. Shock set in when the chemistry teacher asked me why I was repeating the class. When the above reason was voiced, he proceeded to announce that if he had anything to do with it, I would not get a better grade. My love for fairness kicked in, and I would show him. If I earned the grade, he would have to give the grade. He would not relinquish an A, but had to give me at least a B, which I had well earned.

As I was graduating, I never remember feeling that I had made an inappropriate choice. I don't remember Carole and I ever talking about the fact that we would not be graduating together, which I guess speaks to the level of comfort we had in being true to ourselves as individuals.

College did not come next, even though I was accepted into nursing school in Greenwich, Connecticut. I wanted to get a bachelor of science in nursing and teach. This was runner up to my crushed desire to study medicine. Interestingly, years later, I took a couple of career inventories and teaching headed the list. Through the years, when sitting in many different seminars, I would often find myself thinking I would much rather be conducting the program than sitting in the audience. However, as reality would have it, there was no money for college. The motivation and industriousness that would have been necessary to make it happen, if possible, were missing at that period of my life.

In the 70's and two children later, I did go to Essex College in Baltimore and received an associate's degree in mental health. Aside from having my two sons, this was the happiest time in my life. I loved being in school.

Education after that came in dribs and drabs, here and there, seminar after seminar.

The latest program was at the Washington School of Psychiatry, studying psychotherapy and counseling for the aging. It was a wonderful program with countless benefits.

*by: Carole*

These are the years one would expect to be chock-full of memories. They are the foundation years blending with what one learns from one's home life. It is a time of endless experiences that helps to shape a child's life, with no exceptions.

Franklin Washington Edgar School in Metuchen, New Jersey, was my first experience in attending school. This small school had all the grades in one building. It was not that far from where we lived, and walking to school was okay with the exception of not having an opportunity to ride the big yellow school bus. Even as a small child, there was something about being outside with nature that called to me. Most exciting was we got to go to the same school as our sister, Dawn.

I remember my second grade teacher clearly. She was a friend of Dawn's and later became her sister-in-law. It was fun having her for a teacher, although Mother always claimed that she did not provide the rudiments of reading for us to perform at our peak.

Then there was Suzie, a favored friend. Elaine and I just loved Suzie and playing with her was so, as we would say nowadays, cool. One day, cool little Suzie bit our second grade teacher! Her teeth marks were left on the teacher's arm. Our teacher left that day, never to return. I was overwhelmed by the happening, but we remained friends. Was this an unspoken act of forgiveness?

In these earlier years, Elaine and I were in the same class, so going to school was less intimidating. They did not separate us, and I liked that because I had my sister there to support the awkward moments.

Royal School in Darien, Connecticut, was our second school experience. The school was about three blocks from our home on Mansfield Avenue. I loved walking to school here, too. This was to become the first time that Elaine and I were separated. I didn't want that to happen, but there was no option. We would walk to school together and meet at recess time. This gave me a chance to know that she was not far away. Part of the school grounds had fields of clover that were so pretty. At recess, we would sit in the fields of clover and create these beautiful clover chains that we made into bracelets and necklaces… I still remember the delight in creating this jewelry from nature. During recess, we would also play ball, which I loved to do. I remember field hockey being my very favorite sport over softball. It may seem that we were a little young to be playing field hockey in fifth grade but not so apparently. Then there was the time at the end of the day to reconnect with my sister and walk home together sharing our day's experience. I missed her a lot.

The Farm School in Vineland, New Jersey, is where we attended school when we lived with Aunt Margaret while our parents were on a trip to Texas. (We were there several months.) We went to a little one-room schoolhouse "down the road a piece," as they say in the country. It was unlike anything we were accustomed to, with each row representing a grade. I don't have any further recollection of what we learned in that school, but I remember the little boys. At recess time, they would run after Elaine and me to give us a kiss. On a superficial level, we seemed okay with it. Once again, we were walking to and from school.

The Annex, as it was called, was where only the sixth graders went to school in Darien. Elaine and I were together again, and I loved it so much. I am not certain if it meant as much to her as it did to me. It wasn't because we were twins; it was more about a sense that something was missing in my life. I never knew what it was until I was forty. On my fortieth birthday, it had been revealed we were triplets. As you might imagine it came as quite a surprise. However, my two sisters filled this emptiness for me unknowingly as best as it could be satisfied.

Once again, we were walking to school. We didn't have the grand experience of taking a school bus. I always had a little envy for the kids that did.

Darien Junior High was for seventh, eighth, and ninth grades. We attended the seventh and eighth grades here. Again, we were separated by the dictates of the school system. I remember these as two uneventful years, and I excelled in my studies enough to move graciously on without complications. I also remember typing class and my crush on my teacher, who was Native American. I believe that was my first inkling that I had this passion for the Indian culture. I loved the stories he shared with us.

Then there was my second childhood crush. I just thought Lou was the best. One day when I came to school, I heard that he had died over the weekend from a bee sting while cutting the grass. It was a shock for my tender heart. All I could think about when I heard the news was where Elaine was. I needed her to talk with but had to wait until after school. It didn't seem that anyone even noticed how badly I was hurting. The comfort I was longing for had nothing to do with being twins.

Mother of God Academy in Stamford, Connecticut, was where we attended three quarters of ninth grade. It was my first strong feeling about any of the schools we had attended so far. To me, the others were just schools and part of the growing up process. I had a love hate relationship with MOGA. Have you ever had one of those? I loved it because it was an all-girls school, and that felt like fun to me. I didn't mind learning; I actually liked it. Even further, it brought me closer to a new boyfriend who was in a private school right down the street. Imagine that, right down the street. Now, what kid wouldn't like that? But our stay there was to become bittersweet and short-lived. I found the school to be rigid and strict.

Being accepted into the Academy was to be our first real experience in making our own clothes. So Elaine and I went to the school and saw what the uniforms looked like, and we duplicated them out of yards of navy blue wool. The skirt was to have four box pleats, two in the front and two in the back. Fortunately, the blazer was designed without a collar—a blessing! Nonetheless making the uniforms was no easy feat. We accomplished this with great pride and a little help from our father. Yes, Daddy had four sisters, and he knew how to sew—the king of zippers.

Darien High School was where I spent the last three years of high school. I liked this school experience the best. Darien was a snooty little town, and this became much more apparent in the higher grades. The students of the high-income families ran the student council and other such groups in the school. Fortunately, Elaine and I were always included in the outer circle of the inner circle.

When it came to cheerleading, however, we did not make the grade, and this really disappointed me, although I am not certain about my sister. As time passed, with the disappointment in the forefront of my mind, a friend, my sister, and I developed a twirling squad. There were five of us who practiced in the barn of one of the members who lived on a beautiful estate. When we perfected our performance to where we were proud, we presented it to the school. Having not had a twirling squad before, the squad was accepted with reluctance and a compromise had to be reached on the style of the uniforms. The compromise was between short shirts versus slacks to a skirt midway to the knees. Can you imagine twirling in slacks? At first, the principal of Darien High thought that was a most reasonable request until the twirlers appealed to his usually strong views and convinced him how awkward slacks would be for twirlers. Our choice was skirts that matched the length of the cheerleaders' skirts. Now who could refuse such a compromise?

It was in my sophomore year that I met my very first forever friend. She passed away, much too early. She also was a twin. One day in assembly, I looked around me and saw this girl sitting in the auditorium looking lost and realized I had never seen her before. I kept looking at her until I got her attention and smiled to let her know she wasn't alone. Not long after that smile, she and I became the best of friends—a friendship that lasted long beyond our school days. I loved Judy like a sister.

In our senior year, we moved out of Darien to nearby Stamford. Mother asked the school if we could remain there for our senior year since we had virtually grown up in the Darien School system, and they obligingly said yes. I was caught by surprise when Elaine announced she was going to go to Stamford High School. How could she leave me after all our school years together? Mom did not like that idea and neither did I, for two very different reasons. Nevertheless, Elaine made the move. So we ended all of our school years, the last year, in separate schools. How foreign that felt to me. While we were so independent of the "twinie" thing, she was, nonetheless, my "dear sister friend."

All through high school, I made my own clothes. It was a glorious day when I was voted best dressed, because that meant I could go to the Darien Sport Shop and select a complete outfit. I was so proud and happy. I selected a camel hair suit and brown cashmere sweater. I was also voted most domestic, which I never understood. Perhaps it was because of my sewing talents, but domesticity did not feel like my cup of tea. It was nice to walk away with these honors, which I was totally not expecting.

In my yearbook, one of the captions read "Perpetual Tan." I had an insatiable thirst for being in the sun and looking tan. It was nothing to find me wrapped in a quilt with aluminum foil in hand in the middle of the winter. Elaine would join me on a rare occasion. Oh, to the innocence of youth!

Graduation was bittersweet. Sweet because I could move on to something new in my life, and bitter because I was being sent out into the world to become someone, but I had no idea who. What I did know, was that I was not interested in my only option at that time—enrollment into Katherine Gibbs Secretarial School. Where was my sister, Elaine? I wanted her to be there with me to share in this experience. After all, we had shared the big occasions in life from the beginning until now. But so it was a new beginning.

Fairfield University in Fairfield, Connecticut, was where I went to take several marketing courses along the way that would enhance my work career.

Ministry School in New Britain, Pennsylvania, was my final school up to the age of seventy-one. I graduated as an ordained interfaith minister in May 2011. This was an undeniable calling. I am glad I had the strength and the courage to follow my dream while working full time and visiting my mother in an assisted care home three times a week. It was a lot of driving, a lot of long days, a lot of studying, and a huge commitment. I am forever grateful for the vitality and tenacity it took to accomplish my goal. It was with God's grace only. Amen!

# CAREER DIRECTION
## *by: Elaine*

Elaine and Carole—Corporate Specialties

Where does one's career start? Is it with a sparkle in their parents' eyes as they imagine, *I am going to have a son or daughter who will set the world on fire doing whatever it is their dream for them may be?*

Or does it start when you pick up your baby doll and think about taking care of her, just like you are being taken care of?

Or maybe you find yourself entertaining your parents' friends in song and dance that only your parents can genuinely applaud. Remember Carole's and my "Billy Boy" routine and the singing lessons that followed and the determination that perhaps singing should be put on a back burner for another life?

How about once you are in school and everyone is talking about future interests *or* perhaps you saw a movie of a model walking down a runway looking very sophisticated and beautiful that spoke mountains as to how you wanted to present such an image. Later on, such an opportunity occurred when I was asked to model in a fashion show luncheon at one of Darien's prestigious Country Clubs. Marring the total image of perfection was when the stage director stuffed my very first bra with tissue paper. That was a bit of an ego deflector.

By now, you are probably thinking of other possibilities: like that caring veterinarian who so wonderfully took care of your pet Fido, *or* that counselor at school who made you feel your thoughts and desires were important. Perhaps you could do that for others. See how the list could go on and on with all kinds of scenarios.

Perhaps you had a parent who was a teacher, maybe even a doctor or lawyer who made you feel you needed to commit to a like career. Or maybe you had a parent who missed an opportunity to fulfill their dream career and decided they could live it through one of their children by pushing, mentoring, and in some instances, actually coercing their offspring to go in a specific direction. Alternatively, maybe you or a significant other has suffered a malady that caused you to search the world for answers that you just had to share via the format of a career.

For me, my multifaceted career is ongoing and still evolving. No bells, no whistles, no sparklers just a variety of happenings within life's journey that brought about whatever was needed at a given moment. Rather than ascribing to a career, one might refer to my life as a number of happenings, a mixed bag, and endless journeys.

On my sixteenth birthday, I ventured to Stamford, a nearby town for working papers. Back then, in 1957, working papers were required. I remember getting the bus and feeling as if I was the only person moving around the town. Literally, I was there at the break of dawn anxiously waiting for those official doors of the employment office to open. I had my first job already lined up. Babysitting would now be a task of the past.

Working papers in hand, I headed for The Fabric Barn, in Darien, Connecticut. This was a job made in heaven, for I loved fabrics. The owner told my mother that he felt guilty that I spent most of my earnings on fabrics. When I left that job a year later, my old toy chest was filled with fabrics waiting for design. Carole's was, too; we both had worked there.

When we wanted a new outfit for something, my mom would say, "I'll buy you the material, and you can make it." Sewing came kind of naturally to me as I seamed up skirts, blouses, dresses, and suits, whatever need dictated. By the age of sixteen, I certainly had a handle on sewing. I often wondered how I missed the prospect of fashion design, as I altered patterns and improvised. To this day, I love color and fabrics. Decorating in general gets my attention.

When I left The Fabric Barn, it was to sell ready-made clothing in a small individually owned shop in the same town. I envisioned no more sewing, as I would now be making enough money to buy the real thing. However, as reality would have it, it wasn't quite enough money for my lofty plan. In the process, I realized that retail sales did not necessarily call to me.

I had a short period of working for New England Bell before leaving on the Texas trip that you read about earlier.

There may be a reader or two who remembers the old-fashioned cord boards for processing phone calls, back when party lines were the thing. Here I was a telephone operator for a short period. This was when your headset indicated a call with a ringing sound and you would pick up the appropriate cord, placing it in the appropriate slot, greet the caller, take the associated cord, and plug it into an unlit, outside circuit. When the lights went out indicating the call had ended, you would remove both cords and wait for the next call.

I will never forget one day picking up a call and recognizing the voice on the other end of the line. I wanted to acknowledge my recognition so badly. "Hi, my friend, how are you? Guess who this is!" Professionalism won out as I contemplated just how small our world is.

Next, I found a job with an orthodontist and let my independence show too much. I had met my soon-to-be-husband and planned our marriage date around the dentist's vacation. Of course I would be off from work if he were not there. This was not so. I was given the option to change my plans or put an ad in the paper to hire my replacement. Yes, I did the latter.

Next step was on to American Machine and Foundry Company. This job was acquired through an employment agent that I had convinced to assure the man who would be interviewing me that it would be worth his time at least to meet with me and let me prove my skills, even though I only typed nine words a minute on the typing test. I was a fairly decent typist, but I guess the clunker they gave me to type on with a timer at my elbow was not conducive to speed. The agency said it was pointless, but I had confidence in my skills, and by the end of the day, after an agreed-upon interview, I found myself manager of AMF's blue print department. Once again, it was hardly my aspiration!

What *was* my aspiration?

After a rather successful year, I left AMF in Connecticut and headed to Texas with my service husband. He was being relocated, and that meant moving.

The next period in my life was consumed with moving from Texas, to Georgia to Connecticut to Pennsylvania. I held varied short-term jobs and had my two sons.

## MY TWENTIES:

- *Highlights*
  1962—My first son, Stephen, was born in Savannah, Georgia—happiest moment in my life.

1966—My second son, Richard, was born in Timonium, Maryland—second happiest moment in my life.

- *Lived in* Texas, Georgia, Connecticut, New Jersey, and Maryland

- *Employment*
Optical Company in Abilene, Texas
    A temporary position
About Faces in Baltimore, Maryland
    entrepreneurial position-cosmetic company
Romper Room in Towson, Maryland
    This was kind of interesting in that I helped to write and schedule scripts for Romper Room throughout the world. The Klasters also owned Duck Pins and Dollars. Burt and Nancy Klaster and their daughter, "Miss Sally," were great people to work with.

Avon, in Baltimore, Maryland
    Back then, selling Avon meant going door-to-door. I saw it as a way to meet people, determine my own hours, and enjoy a good product. Most importantly, it allowed me to be home with my children.

Depositions, typing for a court reporter in Towson, Maryland
    I did this work at night so I would be home with my sons during the day. In the process, I learned to read the steno tapes and, for a moment, contemplated becoming a court reporter. I determined that using a stenotype machine and an electric typewriter typing tapes was just too tedious. For those unfamiliar typing on a stenotype machine, it is like typing chords and requires a speed of close to 300 wpm. Continually switching techniques was rather challenging.

I took a course to be a court reporter. I finished the course, which was not for naught as I used my learned skill to transpose court-reporting tapes into typewritten reports. This saved the court reporter from having to dictate her work, and increased my income.

## MY THIRTIES

- *Highlights*
1970s: going to college, at last. I got an associate of arts in mental health with extended courses. I absolutely loved being in school.

- *Lived in* Maryland and Pennsylvania

- *Employment*
Monumental Properties in Baltimore, Maryland
Credit and Collection Manager
   This position brought about a learning experience. I was in need of employment and was told repeatedly that I was over-qualified. I did not relate to that concept. When one needs a job, being over-qualified doesn't necessarily fall into the equation. Nonetheless, that was the frequent response, so I decided to turn things around. I placed an ad in the paper, listing my qualifications and interest in employment. In less than a week, I was managing a credit and collection office of four. Having never been in collections before, I developed my own technique applying my psychology background and uncovered many thousands of dollars in a short amount of time. While there, I got an offer to work as a therapist in Children Services in Baltimore, Maryland. (That is what I had

gone to school for and where I had done one of my practicums). I could not say no.

Baltimore Mental Health Clinic—Inner City Catchment area in Baltimore, Maryland
Therapist in Children Services—
This position was just what I wanted; however after a year, I could not afford to stay there. Our department was working on a grant, and it did not provide enough for me to meet my financial responsibilities.
Sprint Telecommunications in Baltimore, Maryland and Philadelphia, Pennsylvania
Hired, trained, and wrote scripts for residential services. During a sales moratorium, I spent a year at the corporate headquarters in Burlingame, California

MCI Telecommunications in Bala Cynwyd, Pennsylvania
Outside professional telecommunications marketing and sales

## MY FORTIES

- *Highlights*
Years of expressing entrepreneurial desires
- *Lived in* Pennsylvania
- *Employment*
Telecomputer Research, Inc. in Bala Cynwyd, Pennsylvania
Co-owned and ran a telecommunications-consulting firm, Telecomputer Research, Inc., TRI
Bala Cynwyd, Pennsylvania
Corporate Specialties in Bala Cynwyd, Pennsylvania
Entrepreneurial endeavors

Carole and I started this company that offered corporate services. Initially, we offered professional shoe shining. We had college students who went into corporate offices and shined executives' shoes. We refurbished an antique bootblack stand we contracted to put in a Best Western Hotel on City Line in Bala Cynwyd, Pennsylvania and established a European shoe-shining service at the Marriott in Center City, Philadelphia. Our motto: "You Scuff Them, We Buff Them." We lacked the funds to grow the business, and it came to a screeching halt.

Modeling in Bala Cynwyd, Pennsylvania

Signed up with an agency in Philadelphia and was putting together a portfolio when the photographer left the area with most of my proofs—never to be located.

Testing Software in Bala Cynwyd, Pennsylvania

I enjoyed testing software for user friendliness, but position was sporadic based on need.

Interior Decoration in Blue Bell, Pennsylvania

I truly loved decorating—I never knew what time it was, but to continue, I would have had to start my own business, and in that field you need dependable, quality fabricators and installers. Again, capital was an issue.

## *MY FIFTIES*

- *Highlights*

Jack was looking for my twin without even knowing I had a twin! And he found her. Carole moved to Pennsylvania.

- *Lived in* Pennsylvania

- *Employment*

  The Fabric Store in Blue Bell, Pennsylvania

  > After searching for a company to support in home decorating and not finding one I wanted to align myself with, I did take a position doing outside decorating for a local fabric store. I was forced to leave there, because our ethical values did not match.

  Financial Corporation in Devon, Pennsylvania

  > Part time and temporary employment

  Hydro Components in Blue Bell, Pennsylvania

  > Division manager for sanitary heat exchangers developing and executing the marketing and sales approach. Major customers were power plants and paper mills. This company was an affiliate to the company that hired Carole—we had adjoining offices. One day Carole brought us lunch. We decided to eat at our respective desks in our adjacent offices. About half way into my lunch, working as I ate, I all of a sudden had this major hot flash and sense of passing out. I went to Carole's door and questioned her sense of well-being, and she was just starting to have a similar response. Long story short, we were both having an allergic reaction to the spelt in the pasta.

  Rogers, Page & Associates in Norristown, Pennsylvania

  Husband's Law Firm

  > As Hydro Components was closing down, my husband was needing a secretary and asked me to fill in for a couple of weeks until he could find someone. This administrative position lasted four years.

# *MY SIXTIES*

- *Highlights*
  My first book was published, May 2011

  *"and then there was me" living with a dying loved one*

- *Lived in* Pennsylvania

- *Employment*
  Kilcoyne & Nesbitt Law Firm in, Blue Bell, Pennsylvania
  > Legal secretary, to one of the partners, I took the position, through an employment agency, not wanting to work in a law firm, but said I would help. I was asked to reconsider permanent employment. I accepted and ended up losing the job because of needs in caring for my sick husband.

  The Path—entrepreneurial
  > This was a rewarding experience helping individuals and corporations design mission and vision statements. Carole, my son, Stephen, and I worked together presenting seminars based on *The Path*®.

  ACTS Retirement Life, Lansdale, Pennsylvania
  > Found this job after a year of looking with no success. I was sixty-five and absolutely knew that age was a factor. The same day of my interview, I was offered the position of Administrative Assistant to the Senior Vice President of Sales and Marketing. It was perfect for my circumstances and me. My ill husband was in a nearby nursing home, which made it very convenient.

  Premier Jewelry—entrpreneurial
  > I sold bridge/high fashion jewelrly as a side endeavor—actually, more as an interest introduced to me by my daughter-in-law, Joan.

Caregiver to my husband of twenty years

I never viewed myself as a caregiver, but that is semantics. It was like having a second job.

## *MY SEVENTIES*

- *Highlight*

  Meeting my wonderful, caring, accepting, and supportive partner—retiring and moving to DC

- *Lived in* Pennsylvania and Washington, DC

  I have been blessed with an adaptable spirit and have been very happy in DC despite the many changes. My ninety-eight-and-a-half-year-old mother passed away two months before I retired and moved. I would not have made the change while she was still living. DC offers so much for a searching soul.

- *Endeavors*

  School

  I am taking a Certification program at the Washington School of Psychiatry: Psychotherapy and Counseling of the Aging. Again I am loving being in school.

  Authoring

  Writing the book that you are now holding in your hands

I have always been an entrepreneurial spirit. At this point, I really don't expect that to change, nor would I want it to. I am developing a program and workshop that will help those who are care giving to find constructive support and hope. As people are living longer, the need for encouragement, support, assessment, and education in this area are growing rapidly.

I am very anxious to devote time and experience to the village concept of aging in place. Incorporated in the above program will be a developed plan to help people in planning their last rites, as it is their right. It will stress the need for communication and appropriate action.

*by: Carole*

When I was really young, I had a fascination for medicine and how it seemingly would heal people, especially people that I loved. This fascination would change later in my life to the holistic approach; of course, there is a place for traditional medicine as well. This unfaltering fascination created a desire in me to be a nurse when I grew up. As the adolescent years passed, I had a desire to have a happy family with a husband and a few children, living in a sweet little house on a corner property with a white picket fence and beautiful roses adorning the yard. How beautiful that thought felt to me. It seemingly superseded all else.

It makes me recall this one day in my senior year of high school in the girls' room; everyone was talking about meeting doctors and lawyers and I quite indignantly thought, *Doesn't anyone want love?* It was at that moment I thought rather profoundly that I would like to have one man and one family for the rest of my life. That was more important than anything else. As irony would have it, several in that conversation ended up in my perfect scenario, except me.

I am not certain when it was that I thought about my life in terms of a career. However, my work career began almost the day I turned sixteen. I worked for the Darien Textile Barn, bringing my wages home in material to make the clothes I wore in high school.

This was the beginning of feeling responsible for myself, and it came with a certain amount of pride that I could maybe do it.

Upon graduation from high school, I worked for New England Bell Telephone for a few months. One day at work, I picked up a coin box call and recognized a voice. After stating where he was calling, I said, "Is that you, David D?" He asked, "How would you know that?" I responded, "I just do." And that was that. It was just a short-lived job.

I believe my serious career life started when I embarked on a runaway trip to Texas shortly after graduating from high school.

## *MY TWENTIES*

- *Highlights*
  1960—My first baby girl, Susan, was born with beautiful red hair. I was in love.
  1965—My second baby girl, Dawn, was born with beautiful brunette hair. I was in love all over again.

- *Lived in* Connecticut and Maryland

- *Employment*
  Not long after I returned to Connecticut, I entered the dental arena. I liked this work very much, because helping people to find comfort while at the dentist seemed important to me, and performing a job that brought me a satisfactory income considering I had not gone onto further education at this time was a blessing. Gratefully, the first dentist I worked for trained me to be his assistant. I did this for several years and moved on to working for a dental surgeon for a year before going on to becoming a legal secretary. It was a bittersweet journey, for I was to find that it caused me a health concern.

  Back in the 1960s, the amalgam fillings were in vogue, and as an assistant, you would twist the mercury out of the amalgam for the dentist to import to the tooth of the not so fortunate, totally unaware recipient—unaware of the negative effects of amalgam fillings. At that point in time, the assistants did not wear gloves in the line of duty. As the years passed, I came to find that mercury exposure coupled with the amalgam fillings in my teeth created a very high level of mercury in my body. I was grateful that with much research and diligent dieting, I was able to bring the high levels of mercury down to a more tolerable level.

Just before starting employment as a legal secretary, I found myself in labor for the second time, with a 105 degree fever and pneumonia. The doctor announced that he did not know how things would go and if necessary to make a decision, what would I want. "Me or the baby?" Was I hearing him correctly as these words resounded in my head causing me to feel more sick than I was already? I found myself wishing my sister was there. We always talked when things were serious and I needed to talk with her now. That was sadly not possible. Of course the answer was easy… save the baby. Suddenly in the midst of this nightmare, a miracle filled my experience and my fever broke just long enough for labor. My little girl was whisked away to an incubator to match my body heat and to bring it down gradually, and me to a private room away from others. When Elaine got there to see me, she walked right by my room. I saw her and wondered where she was going. She did not recognize me. My face was swollen from the pneumonia and I understood this when I was able to get up and look at myself in the mirror. I let out a scream of shock. I didn't recognize me either.

I enjoyed working in the legal office. It was a little more challenging than the dental experience and a different kind of socialization with the clients. I have always loved communicating with others and hungered yet for more challenges. While it seemed ideal in many ways, I was being forced to relocate due to expenses. I made the decision to afford my two daughters and myself a short interlude to Baltimore. I moved in with Elaine and her husband to see if there was anything in that area for me. I contacted an employment agency and was sent out on a couple of fruitless interviews and called one more time and asked them to consider something else.

The recruiter came back to me and said, "When you hear a famous name do you get excited?" I responded, "Try me." She asked, "Do you know Brooks Robinson (hall of fame 3rd baseman for the Baltimore Orioles)?" I answered, "No, who is he?" Then she said, "You are just the girl for the job" and sent me for the interview.

I walked in for the interview. Little did I know, the job offer was minutes away. Two brothers who ran the business thought I would be a perfect fit. I stayed awhile, but the job did not pay enough for my little girls and me to move into our own place. I wanted to leave my sister's gracious hospitality for a life of our own. We moved back to Connecticut. I did not have the proper schooling nor was I prepared for the outside world singly raising two children. However, I had a strong sense of independence and responsibility.

## *MY THIRTIES*

- *Highlights*
  1970—My third baby girl, Cheryl, was born with beautiful brown eyes, and for the third time, I fell in love all over again
  1978—I developed a skin care product and founded a company, Vivante, with two partners.

- *Lived in* Connecticut

- *Employment*

  I found a position in an allergist's office and came to like this position a lot and began to see myself there for some time. The office would close for two hours at lunch, and I delighted in the opportunity to read by the water. Then one day, the doctor, who claimed to be my father-like figure, called me in and gave me one month to find another job. He said, "You won't understand this now, I know, but I believe in my heart of hearts this is best for you and your daughters." He felt it would give me a chance to make more money than he felt he could ever pay me and a chance to meet a potential partner perhaps. I went home that evening believing my whole world had been turned upside down.

  I did not have the vaguest idea how I was going to pull it all together. The girls and I were accustomed to our economic conditions. Although not great, we were, nonetheless, on our own. I did not want to leave. However, he was unrelenting about his decision.

  I heard about a corporation in the area that may be looking for someone, thanks to my mother's bridge world. She was a life master bridge player, and I knew all the players. One of the men who played on her team came to mind, and he set me up for an appointment at Olin in Stamford. It was in the top Fortune 500, and the opportunity seemed perfect. I was instantly hired and ended up working for just short of ten years with this corporation. It was quite a climb up the corporate ladder. I started as an administrative support secretary and knew when customer service was centralized into corporate headquarters, I would want to become director of customer service for the industrial division. I had energetic dreams for my future. The director had another plan for me knowing that I would be a perfect candidate for that position. I did set my goal with tunnel vision. It meant working in the ranks of scheduling, in house sales/customer service to get to the top.

It turned out to be a journey laced with great joy and some fear. Great joy because I did well and experienced a raise and new position every six to nine months. My boss told me this was unheard of in a major corporation, but nonetheless it was happening and I was driven. I knew God was gracing my world with these rewards—heaven only knows how much I needed them in raising my girls. And fear because of the corporate games a single woman had to face in that particular environment—games I was not willing to play. I simply could not play the game; it went against my very core. However, in the midst of the corporate politics, I was honored for having developed a division-wide standardization program to keep things seamless for the customers when there were absentees in the department. My customers were like my babies, and I wanted them to be nurtured as much as possible when I was not there, hence the system for this was born and gratefully embraced by the department. I also created a nationwide satellite customer service club for managers from other major corporations to come together, share, and learn from their experiences, thus affording the possibility to develop a customer service department that would function second to none. I knew early on that the heartbeat of any successful business is the customer.

Only one promotion away from the director position, I was moved to the training department. I was to put together a program to teach one hundred forty people how to do pricing on the new computer system. I knew nothing about computer systems, but I knew how to pray, and I was divinely led on how to get the job done. I successfully did just that. The director had put this seemingly impossible challenge in front of me. He wanted me out of customer service. I would later make the decision to leave this corporation on my own accord.

During my years there, I was also a liaison to many departments and got to know the marketing team as well. One gentleman said to me one day, "I love your enthusiasm in life, and if you ever come up with anything, bring it to me." He was aware of my entrepreneurial spirit.

One day, in the midst of my corporate career, I came to my friend with a product I had developed on the side. It was a skin care product. I didn't mind the maturing process, but I wanted to look as good as I could for as long as I would live. I had gone to About Faces in Baltimore, Maryland, studied the skin, and came up with a product so pure you could eat it on your salad—literally! He was so impressed with the results of my blind sample studies that he set up an appointment with a friend of his in the product formulation area of a major corporation. Because of the meeting, we started our company Vivante Products. We three made a great team—my product, my one partner's marketing expertise, and my other partner's product development skills. We were all full-time employees of major corporations, but on Thursday evenings, we would meet at the Ryetown Hilton Hotel where we developed our exclusive business plan, designed our marketing strategy, and created a beautiful packaging for our elegant product. After successfully developing, packaging, and selling the first two thousand pieces, we took our business plan to a venture capital group in New York City. We had claim substantiation, which was beyond our wildest dream—we found that the product had two more substantiated claims than the highly unlikely seven we presented. With this information, we introduced our product to the capital group, and much to our surprise, we were offered three million dollars with one hitch—all three would be full time employees of Vivante. My partners were not going to be able to leave their jobs, and so we needed to turn the offer down. This perhaps was one of the biggest disappointments in my life and perhaps one of the greatest lessons. When we formed the partnership, I thought it was fair for us to be equal one-third partners since we all brought our expertise to the project that made it a complete package. I found that when it is your product, you always need controlling interest, even if it is only by one percent.

# MY FORTIES

- *Highlights*
  1987—I took a sabbatical from the work world and traveled in Europe for 2 years.
  1980s—Life blessed me with five magnificent grandchildren: two girls and three boys—Ashley, Zachery, Samantha, Mario, and Michael. The wonder of a grandchild is a magical and blessed event.
  1980s—I can't forget to mention my sweeter than ever grand-dogs, Beau and Sadee.

- *Lived in* Pennsylvania and Connecticut

- *Employment*
  As my career in Corporate America ended, I found myself moving to Philly to be part of my sister and her husband's business in the telecommunications industry. The job was in marketing and sales. Though not my cup of tea, I somehow found that I did very well in sales types of jobs. I never felt that my creativity was being expressed. My daughter pointed out to me, "You are a people person; hence, you do well because your customers know you care and want the best for them." I knew my customers trusted me.

  During this time in the Philly area, the bug bit again to go into something of my own. The entrepreneurial spirit had kicked in. I found myself day dreaming about this little shoe-shine man who walked the floors of Olin, in his quiet unassuming way shining shoes for the top executives and their secretaries, even while they were in meetings. When he passed away, I remembered reading how he left a million dollars to his beloved family as well as having put two children through college. The wheels of my mind were churning with excitement as to what I could do with this *idea*. I went to my sister, Elaine, and Corporate Specialties was born.

Under the company umbrella would be a shoeshine service. We would set up three to five corporations a day to serve each day of the week. While this would be a cash and carry business, we knew if we could get the clientele established in each company, we could train a person to go with a required goal and then we would have to trust in the balance of the business. Setting up the corporation for this service was an easy sale. Our enthusiasm was shining through. In addition to the corporations, we contracted with a hotel in the local area to pick up the guests' shoes late at night and return them in the wee hours of the morning—European style. Also, we contracted for a bootblack stand in a center-city hotel. Everything was falling into place successfully when all of a sudden my sister's husband announced his big problem with our project. He did not want his wife or her look-alike running around corporations shining shoes. Now this would have been essential to get the business established. After much discussion, it was decided that we would put our project to rest. This was so hard to do. It was a staggering business plan and would have been an incredible business.

In the wake of this disappointment, I looked at the possibility of going into recruiting with Snelling & Snelling, one of the world's largest employment firms for office services. That is what I did. Fortunately, I fell into this position with great ease. It was the first time in my work career that I would be on straight commission. That was a little scary, but I knew I could do it. Not long into the job, I became dissatisfied working with office service applicants. I wanted to work with management-level positions since that was my background. I stayed for a while, nonetheless, looking forward to learning about the industry. I ended up with an 80 percent fill ratio, which was considered exceptional. I believe I was able to achieve this because I have an intuitive sense, and most times, I could tell if it was going to be a perfect match. I let the matches happen effortlessly. Half way through my career I was diagnosed with multiple sclerosis, which was expected to be a serious health concern.

It is the strangest feeling to go to bed thinking you are perfect and waking with little feeling on one side of your body below the waist. I called the chiropractor thinking my back was out of alignment, which seemed like a plausible possibility. However, I could not feel the ground under my right foot and that was disconcerting. I called Elaine and we agreed that I needed to see the chiropractor and then make another determination if necessary. The chiropractor sent me to a neurologist for evaluation.

The MRI was completed and the time for results to be given had come. As I entered the neurologist's office she said, "Good morning. You have MS and you will be in the hospital twice a year on cortisone." I was stunned and found the presence within myself to wonder, *What kind of a greeting is this?* As I looked at the empty chair next to me, it didn't seem right that I was sitting there alone hearing this heart-wrenching news. Something came over me and I looked back at the doctor and said, "No, no, I will not." I got up, walked out of her office and perfunctorily paid my bill and boarded the elevator for the ground floor.

Well, I lost it on the ride down from the eighth floor, but as I stepped off the elevator, grateful for the time to get my composure, a peace washed over me and I knew I was going to be alright. I called Elaine immediately and I knew she was stunned too. She assured me we would work it out. Somehow hearing her words and the words of my inner voice I didn't doubt it. I was going to be just fine. I was so sure of this that I went back to work that afternoon with the conviction to learn all I needed to know about MS coupled with my faith would be the answer. Dawn also was to play an important role in helping find the information I needed to know. I was so very grateful for her help.

From the onset, I clearly decided it would not be an issue for me, and so it has not been. That was some thirty years ago.

It was not long after that I met a gentleman and left my job to build a life with him. We ended up traveling in Europe for about two years. It was a glorious two years, and I so enjoyed our travels. What an education to learn about the different cultures first hand. When our travels to the other side of the world ended, so did our relationship. I went back to Connecticut and went to work as an independent contractor / headhunter. Again, I was on straight commission. I had become okay with that—life was good. However, at that point in time, things were changing in the employment industry. Permanent placements were being replaced with temporary placements, and the recruiting world was not as lucrative.

## *MY FIFTIES*

- *Highlights*
  1993—Joined Klenzoid Equipment Company
- *Lived in* Connecticut and Pennsylvania

- *Employment*

  In spite of the turn, things were going along, and I had decided to hang in there with the recruiting. There was a reward in it for me. I was always happy to think that I had helped someone find a job, that brought security to one's life, and satisfaction to an employer. It was win-win-win, and I liked that. Then one day, Elaine called from Philadelphia and said that the parent company to her company was looking for someone in the marketing area. My soon-to-be-boss asked Elaine if she knew of anyone like herself, and she said, "As a matter of fact I do, and not only is she like me but she has a chemical background." I was offered a position with the Klenzoid Equipment Company in Blue Bell, Pennsylvania, and I accepted.

## *MY SIXTIES*

- *Highlights*

  2000s—Authored my first book: *A Closer Walk with God*

  2000s—Formed a partnership with Aaron Graves, a gifted musician, for developing an audiobook.

- *Lived in* Pennsylvania

- *Employment*

  While working at Klenzoid, other areas of my life began to take flight. I wanted to fulfill my dream on a personal level in ways that I had never been able to because of being a caregiver to my parents for many years, helping my family when a need would arise, and just being responsible to myself.

  One day, quite by surprise, life presented me an opportunity to study Reiki. I asked what this healing modality called Reiki was. I needed to understand more, because it seemed to be calling to me. I studied and learned about its beautiful innocent process in the holistic and healing arena. I fell in love with the idea that one day I would become a Reiki Master and bring healing to those who are hurting. As I made the decision to move forward, realizing it was something I had to do, I studied levels one and two. As the years went by, I heard of a Reverend Hannelore Goodwin, a 5th generation Reiki Master, and knew I needed to study Reiki with her. I did just that and became a Reiki Master.

I was beginning to find myself after all these years. I was feeling good, in spite of having to work full-time. I knew I must stay responsible and continue to work as I had been doing. I would be shown the way if I were to make a change. What was different, I knew I needed to continue this exploration in fulfilling my dream.

Then one morning as I was lying in bed, I asked the question to God; we talked every day. I asked, "If I could have spoken to my parents as an unborn child, what would I have asked them to give me coming into this world," and the words just flowed. I took these words and created my first book, *A Closer Walk with God*, to share with those drawn to its pages. Elaine, the beautiful sister friend that she is, was so significant in helping me complete the pictures for the book and the sales.

It was heartwarming when several of my readers came to me and said the book needed to be in audio format. I prayed on this, and one night almost six months since that idea had been presented to me, I met the man who would ultimately partner with me. His soulful style on the keyboard at a jazz evening touched me deeply. At intermission, Aaron Graves and I spoke, and I came to find he is a gifted musician, director, composer, and producer. He fell in love with my book and felt the calling to be a part of the project. Hence, Divine Reflections was founded to grow and prosper giving back to life by its very nature. An English audio book is currently in the works. One will follow soon after in Spanish. Thank you, God, you are amazing.

## *MY SEVENTIES*

- *Highlights*
  2011—Graduated from Interfaith Ministry School
  2011—Certified as a Reiki Master
  2012—Founded two companies:
  > Divine Reflections
  > Once in a Lifetime: Ministry Services

- *Lived in* Pennsylvania

- *Employment*
  Several years followed, and I heard about Circle of Miracles Ministry, a non-denominational school where I could go part-time and graduate as an ordained, interfaith minister. I made the decision to do this. It would allow me to do weddings and life celebrations, and it would be important to my Reiki practice. I knew with certainty that this was the direction I needed to follow. I was working full-time at my job and caring for a 97-year-old mom. School was an hour away, and Mom was forty minutes away in another direction, but I knew I could do it. It was an inner calling. Mother met my decision with reluctance, but I assured her she would see me no less than three times a week. It wasn't long before she greeted me with a smile and was proudly telling everyone what I was doing. She

wasn't able to make the graduation ceremony. However, right after, Mother was surrounded by me and four other graduates with whom I had become close to tell her all about the graduation. She was so delighted, and I was filled with gratitude.

I am currently planning to present seminars to inspire and enhance one's journey in seeking for greater awareness and self-expression. It is one's birthright to live life as your authentic self. These seminars are being designed to include Emotional Freedom Techniques as well.

I am still working in my full-time job with Klenzoid Equipment Company until the time when I will move on to my new calling—that of author, reiki master, interfaith minister, and seminar leader. I want to: savor the projects with Divine Reflections, embrace my Reiki practice on a greater level, pursue my ministry services as they unfold, and work on presenting life-changing seminars. For these gifts to give, I am so divinely blessed.

I have been blessed with the energy and sense of commitment to reach for the stars. I move in the realm of responsibility and possibility, never letting go of my dreams. It is with this commitment and God's grace that I am where I am today. My cup runneth over. Amen.

# TASTE & STYLE
### by: Elaine

When I think of one's taste and style, I think of elements that outwardly define us. Based on that thought, I have always been interested in the differences Carole and I have expressed in this area.

Certainly, in early years, choices are limited by that which is presented to us. However, once able to make your own purchases, those choices grow and develop. It is actually, on some level, a very freeing experience that expands with time, information, observations, and finances. I don't believe I would consider it an innate or genetic process for the most part.

## Clothing

I first became aware of my love for fabric and design when I started sewing and making my own clothes. Natural fibers are by far my favorite—silks, cotton, linen, wool, and blends. At the very top of my list is summer weight wool, which is hard to find. It's cool or warm, does not wrinkle, and drapes beautifully. A sophistocated look in clothing is great—tailored and smooth.

I remember buying a pink blouse with ruffles when I was quite young after the high school years. Each time I put it on, it came right back off; a new blouse was given away. The ruffles were distracting and the color pink was off my list. For some reason the idea of pink for girls and blue for boys never resonated with my senses.

Speaking of dress, one might see ruffles as feminine. My perception is that femininity is innate. Either you have it or you don't. It can be created only to a degree, because once you start moving, it speaks for itself. If you have it, you can exude its wiles even in a trench coat.

At one period in my life, thirties to forties, scarves were a signature item for me, kind of as a tie is to a man. They were flowing out of my dresser drawer. Accessorizing is an important factor to the well-dressed look. Representing a jewelry line for a number of years, I was led to believe seven pieces of jewelry (white gold for me) is the magic number. Sounds like a lot, doesn't it? Not so when you start to count. I usually wear three rings (one being a thumb ring), a watch, a bracelet, and earrings. I also enjoy an anklet, being one who has never liked hosiery.

My work path led me to wear suits, which I find most comfortable. Since I have retired slacks and jeans have been added to the mix. Skirts are a favorite, from tailored to flowing, with eclectic choices of tops.

## At Home

Decorating a home is as interesting and important as decorating myself. However, in a living situation, there are others to consider. I have always had a dream, never fulfilled, to have one room that is mine to decorate just as I would like it to be in total.

Over the years, when finances allowed, I did enjoy decorating in a very traditional style: hardwood floors, oriental carpets, antique furnishings, fine art, shelving for my books and music, lovely flowers, all with some eclectic touches and few, if any, knick knacks. I like the idea of visual surprise—the unexpected in both color and design.

For me, design stems from a feeling, a sense of balance and flow not always easily described.

Once, when chairing a group that refurbished our church sanctuary and renovated the basement into classrooms and social hall, I felt rather challenged. There was so much diverse input, and of course, in honoring the majority, on occasion, I disagreed with the popular vote. That's life!

One thing that became very important to me over the years was recognizing my opinion as valuable as another's and not being intimidated by being different. Perhaps that's the individuality quotient at work.

## About Me and Men

You can't talk about lifestyle and not mention men. Honesty is the most crucial ingredient in any relationship. If you have honesty, then there is trust and love. Those are the basics. Another ingredient critical to a meaningful lasting relationship is respect. To respect and be respected allows for open communication. Realizing each can move to their own drummer and still come back to their special meeting point over and over again allows for a grand connection.

Also important is having sensitivity to another's desires. I believe in giving and receiving, which if based on love and respect, needs no percentage attached.

When giving comes from the heart, the act or art of receiving is a gift returned. On a practical level, I enjoy sharing many activities—theater, dining out, movies, musical events of all kinds, visiting museums, touring new areas, going back to areas to reminisce, art shows, antiquing, walking, swimming, skating, watching a sunset, watching sports, the list could go on and on.

## Lifestyle

Lifestyle in some ways changes with our experiences as we journey through the years.

However, there are constants. My Christian faith is the basis of who I am and what I believe, and it dictates for what I strive. Strive is the operative word in recognizing the human element.

My faith was all-encompassing a number of years ago when I took care of my husband of twenty years for six years before he died. He was very ill, and our journey was very challenging. My faith clearly supported me in every aspect of that journey. After he passed, I found myself waning away from responding actively/formally to my faith, but not in my beliefs. My belief system remains very much intact.

Carole and I were baptized Episcopalian and raised eclectic. Over the years, I have visited the Methodist, Congregational, Presbyterian, Unitarian, Lutheran, and Pentecostal churches, and was baptized again in the Baptist Church, where I spent twenty years and still have my membership.

My parents were not churchgoers, but they insisted that we attend church. At a certain point, it could be any church of our choosing as long as we went. My father would take us and pick us up. I only remember my parents going to church with us on one occasion when I was making a presentation at a Congregational church where I had elected to go for a while.

I never doubted my faith, but I had many questions that didn't get answered until years later by a very astute Lutheran minister that I met. That was somewhat life changing for me as he gave me reassurance that questioning was good and not deviant. I always wondered over the years if others had questions, too. It never looked like they did.

I find it interesting to realize that it never occurred to me to check with Carole about her thoughts and wonderings. Perhaps she didn't have any unanswered questions, but I would not have known.

Were we so busy being independent that we neglected to relate at times?

Were we so busy being independent that we missed out on a level of companionship?

Were we so busy being independent that we really didn't get to enjoy being a "twinie"?

During the years my sons were growing up, I tried to relay the importance of the concept of "marching to your own drummer." I respect one's right to their view and style, whatever it may be, knowing that I don't have to agree and only ask for the same in return.

My friends vary considerably, and I value each immensely. Each friend is unique and so is each relationship. That makes me a great benefactor.

If one comes from a caring and compassionate heart, life works.

Speaking of life, I am a lover of birthdays. Perhaps it started with Christmas. I really don't know when it started, but I do know the joy that comes from recognizing the importance of another in my life. There is a sentimental aspect to a birthday of someone you know. It is the day when their being entered the sphere in which you exit. I don't have a greater explanation, nor do I have greater joy than in celebrating another's life.

As I have journeyed through the years, I keep learning. There are a couple of lessons I would like to share at this juncture.

1. After evaluating the pros and cons of a decision, there are a couple questions to ask yourself. One, which decision will bring you the least regrets; and two, regardless of the outcome, will you be at peace with your choice? There are times when no option feels right; however, one will always bring you fewer regrets. Within a stressful moment of decision making, it may feel that there could be no peace in any decision. Peace will come if you allow yourself to see what the circumstances afford you and know that you are making the best decision within your ability.

2. The importance of receiving graciously: there are many who enjoy giving and many who enjoy receiving. Are you able to do both well? I have heard many speak of the difficulty in receiving more than giving. Those who have expressed this tend to be givers. I have come to realize that when you receive graciously, you are actually giving a gift back to the giver.

My passion in life is to exhibit and promote fairness with compassion and humility.

"What is required of one? "… to be fair and just and merciful and to walk humbly with your God" Micah 6:8 (TLB).

---

*by: Carole*

## Clothing

I don't know exactly when it is in life that your sense of style and your tastes become your very own. I am thinking I was a young adult (mid-twenties), when I realized that inside, I was kind of what might have been called in that era of my life a "flower child." One day I looked at myself—I still remember the moment—I was dressed up in a long, tan, tencel-like skirt with a pretty, white, lacey blouse, and yes black high-top Reebok sneakers, feeling so much like myself that I knew it was me. I loved the skirt because it clung ever so slightly being the nature of that fabric (I love silky fabrics against my skin), coupled with my rather feminine blouse (I love a touch of femininity), topped off with my sneakers ("sneaks"). To me, these sneakers finished my outfit off just perfectly and said to others, "She's really different." Interestingly, today you would think nothing of that sight since we live in a time of growing social acceptance of varying styles, wearing walking shoes with the dress ones in your oversized pocketbook. It was at that defining moment that I knew I needed to dress for me, and to this moment, I have. On a rare occasion, maybe I was pleasing a man in my life with something that pleased me *also*. I have come to a place of not losing myself. This was not surprising because it had become my signature expression from early on.

This thought brings me to a moment when a very nice gentleman that I was dating presented me with a lovely, hot pink, silk blouse. I looked at it and thought he must know something I don't, because my wardrobe was mostly earth tone colors with some whites. I graciously thanked him. Later as I was drifting off to sleep I thought, *What am I going to do with this pink blouse as lovely as it is?* I certainly appreciated its beauty, but it was foreign to my tastes. Yes, I was going to return it to Lord & Taylor. The very next day, standing in Lord & Taylor with blouse in hand, I was swept away with this thought, *This was a gift of love. You need to keep it and wear it.* I exited the store, and to this day, beautiful colors have awakened my closet to new opportunities in dressing.

I have always liked clothes that aren't revealing, but rather slightly suggest femininity. I think that is so much more appealing to the eye. I had clearly decided this when I was spending time in Germany. I thought the style of dress was so lovely, gently soft, and "feminine," a key word to me in dress. Yet, femininity is different to each person. As in life, it is a perception. To me, it was flowing clothes with an ever so slight cling giving a sense of style that was appropriate for the occasion. While I was there, I, without thought, packed my belongings into my suitcase, sent them back to the states, and walked on over to a magnificent boutique. It was owned by a lovely couple who outfitted me with clothes for my stay. I fully loved the experience. There is nothing like feeling beautiful in your clothes. I have since come to believe that, when you are in a loving place within yourself, you will be led to select what makes you feel naturally beautiful.

I believe if you were to ask those who know me how I dress, they would say stylishly conservative—again a perception. I might add that in later years, I have come to love a touch of sparkle not only to my clothes, but also to things in my environment.

**At Home**

In my earlier years, I loved contemporary furnishings. They felt clean, fresh, and open. I did not like to feel confined. I have always loved the feeling of spaciousness, and still do. I loved whites and grays with touches of color to accent. My first condominium, I decorated every room in a true gray (as you know all colors have tones of other colors, warm or cool, but each has a true color on the chart as well). The different rooms were accented in peach, almond, black, and silver with touches of red and merlot. People would come into my home and say it looked like it belonged in Better Homes & Gardens Magazine. It didn't make that venue, but it did appear in the Philadelphia Inquirer Magazine section as "Place" of the week. Thank you, Ellen Kaye.

As the years go by, we collect items, and we are given lovely gifts that also fill our space. I would say my style has evolved to a more traditional style with a touch of contemporary, and my love for the Oriental and Native American cultures has brought special items relating to these cultures into my home. The color pallet of my home has evolved also to deeper richer tones. But more important to me is the energy in my home. I love when people walk in and tell me my home is peaceful. That is my dream for them to feel. We personally bring to our environment what we are feeling, because life is energy. And for those who are kinesthetic or first feeling, what better than to feel peace? We all are kinesthetic, visual, and auditory—one being more predominant. Which one are you?

Whether it is in a painting or a statue, there are certain animals that call to me for very decided reasons. I love the panda because it is black and white, the spectrum of the human race as one. I love the giraffe, because it holds its head up high above the others. I love the horse, because it is so majestic and beautiful. Lastly, I love both the lion and the lamb, because they are both biblical and reveal how strength and gentleness can lie down together.

Art touches my soul in so many ways and I try to have special pieces throughout my home.

## About Me and Men

Like any passionate woman, I like men. I am certain that earlier on in my life I was drawn to the men that were drawn to me. I must admit I was looking for love in all the wrong places. I was raised to believe that intimacy came *only* after marriage. This came not only from my upbringing but also from my religion. We were raised High Episcopalian. At sixteen years old, my mother felt she had done her job in seeing that we had a religious education, and she set us free, so to speak. One day she said, "Find a Church that feels comfortable to you." I searched and searched, considering many religions and came close both to converting to Judaism and to becoming non-denominational. I deeply believe we are all spiritual beings, and religion is what we practice. While I chose to live a Christ-conscious life, I do honor each person for what he/she chooses to believe.

One might wonder about the men in the lives of identical twins. Often you hear that twins have married another set of twins or that they have married brothers. This would not be true of this twin set as you might expect, as individual as we were raised and the individuality that we strived for has shown up in the men we have been drawn to. I would say that while we liked each other's choices they clearly would not have been our own.

However, there was one point in our lives we dated "quasi-brothers." I say that in keeping with the African American culture. Coming from a family where diverse cultures were never a topic, this seemed quite unique! Our father passed away before this happening occurred. I am not certain how he would have responded, but it was quite beautiful to see our mother's acceptance. She always maintained that she did not have exposure to diversity nor had she presented that experience to us. So this phenomenon was quite surprising to her.

Nonetheless, she became very close to my boyfriend and to Elaine's husband. Considering the times and the dynamics of interracial relationships, this was quite a gift.

I did come to realize all the love that I would ever need was right here inside of me. It was my walk with God that fulfilled my hunger for love. But as part of the human experience and being the passionate woman that I am, I do want to have a partner in my life. In the earlier days when aesthetics were of greater importance, tall, dark, and handsome (minus a few inches) would have been my first choice. Today, he looks totally different than he looked in the earlier years, because it is about what projects from within. Now, my ideal partner would exude a strong and confident sense of knowing who he is. I would define the perfect relationship for me as one where each of us is free to express fully who we are while honoring the differences in each other, thus creating a place that is safe, warm, peaceful, and loving. This man will be sensitive (willing to be vulnerable), caring, kind, generous, compassionate, and passionate about life. He will be a man of good character, valuing truth and honesty and secure within himself. One day he will say to me, "I cannot imagine my life without you. Your heart is safe with me." This man is going to be my next partner. Many amazing men fill this description; I know some.

**Lifestyle**

Last and certainly not least is my lifestyle. It starts with God first, and walking in faith. Feeding my soul is very important to me. It brings to me a strong sense of who I am. There are several ways I do that. I have found that meditation is such a divine way to be centered and brings that centeredness into my day. I have found that prayer is key to bringing love to me and to those for whom I pray. I have found that it is so important to be your authentic self and I do that in all areas of my life, my home, my office, and my relationships.

Forgiveness is like breathing. It is the very practice that sets you free. I took a course in Radical Forgiveness that brought such compassion to my soul for my mother before she died. We had experienced some difficult years. This felt so beautiful. I cannot imagine forgiveness not being a part of my life. It has become a natural part of my existence.

And gratitude: I emphasize this word because life without gratitude is unimaginable to me. I have been blessed by the grace of God beyond measure. It has brought me to the place I reside in today. I am so grateful. There are two verses in the Bible among many that stand out to me with great reverence: "For He shall give His Angels charge over Thee to keep Thee in all Thy ways" and "Be still and know I am God." And yes, I believe in the stillness that is where I commune with the Creator.

I feed my mind through life experiences and much reading striving to awaken my spirit to even greater heights.

Along with feeding my soul and my mind, I feed my body with my conscious mind. I select foods that will nourish my temple, for that is where my soul resides. Having had several significant health diagnoses, I have come to know that wholeness is a mind-body-spirit connection. Living a holistic lifestyle is a choice we get to make. I have chosen to be a modified vegetarian with great discipline, and it works.

Anything you want to do is easy if it comes from the heart; it is, again, a choice. A very wise man once told me, "If you choose something, and it doesn't feel good, simply choose again." So what is life but choice?

Finally, I live my mission: to reflect, to give of, and to serve from the light within to all who touch my path. If confronted with a life challenge, I simply ask, "What would love do now?" When I live my life from this place, it is a beautiful thing.

# LIVING IN MONTGOMERY COUNTY, PENNSYLVANIA
## *by: Elaine*

Is going back to the area you were born going home? We left Pennsylvania when Carole and I were three, and at thirty-seven, I found myself moving back to Pennsylvania.

Andalusia on the water was a rather nice setting. A year later, my husband and I bought a house in Bala Cynwyd, known as the "main line" area.

We not only moved, we also challenged our entrepreneurial spirits and started a telecommunications consulting firm, still functioning today amidst all the changes that have taken place in the industry and our lives. The company was actually started before the phone company's divestiture in December 1983.

Carole came down to Pennsylvania months later to help with sales, but it took longer than anticipated to grow to the point of supporting a large staff. At that time, we had five people working for us. At one juncture, my oldest son, Stephen, joined the staff on the financial side before going back to complete his last year at Frostburg College.

With the changes in the industry and having to pare down, Carole and I started looking at the possibilities of a unique entrepreneurial adventure.

Eventually Carole went into the corporate workforce with an employment agency and headed back to Darien, Connecticut. I wished she could have stayed, but we needed to keep moving forward with our work efforts and her staying was not in the list of practical options.

However, she did find her way back to Pennsylvania with an employment offer from the company she is still with. The company, Klenzoid Equipment, the one where the owner asked if I knew "someone just like myself" that they could consider hiring.

It is amazing how events in life evolve. I tend to believe what is meant to be, will be. "Que Sera Sera"

On a rare occasion, I would miss Connecticut even though I had not been there for many years. The last time I had lived in Connecticut was when Stephen was a baby and I had left Savannah, Georgia, knowing it was not where I wanted to be. My family shared an apartment with Carole's family for a very short time—weeks not months. Then we moved to Scotch Plains, New Jersey for about a year. That move afforded me the good fortune to be near Dawn and her family for a short time. I really liked getting to know my little niece and nephew better.

An eight year period in Maryland followed my year in New Jersey before moving to Pennsylvania. They were rather tumultuous years, but two events were major highlights for me.

My second son was born. I was delighted and contemplated great things for two instead of one; Stephen and Richard, how blessed I was! I also had the opportunity to go back to school and acquire a degree in mental health and to practice in the field for too short a time. The lack of finances because of working on a grant in children services forced me to find other work.

There is one other major highlight. Do you remember those ice-skating lessons I wanted? I finally took a couple during a lunch hour while working at children services. After two lessons, I was able to do so many of the things I hadn't been able to as a youth. It was all a matter of balance. I realized then that something that seems so simple, perhaps insignificant, can actually be *very* significant. I was anxious to share my finding with Carole as we had spent so many early morning hours, before school, trying to master figure eights and you name it. Rather significant to me was the fact that something as simple as proper balance, which I already thought I had, could make such a difference. Perhaps a lesson there is that the distance between two points may not be as far as they seem.

During my years in Maryland, except for a couple visits, the only time Carole and I saw each other was when I would travel up to Connecticut each month.

Then I moved back to Pennsylvania.

During my time in Pennsylvania, I had to deal with a number of unsettling events. In 1994, I suffered a major subachnroid bleed. Upon arriving in Connecticut for a weekend gathering at my mother's. My life was about to be challenged! The bleed resulted in my being in ICU for a week and almost two weeks in the hospital, later discovering how blessed to have survived the ordeal. Having had short-term memory loss does not allow me to recall that stay in the hospital, but I have heard that my husband, mother, sisters, sons, and other family members were by my side most of the time.

I do have a vague recollection of Carole wanting to be in the emergency room with me and me wanting her there, but the nurse said, "Sloan is in my charge, and I am not going to let anything happen to her." They wouldn't let Carole stay. And I was too sick to appeal as I was drifting in and out of consciousness.

I want to share a story that happened during that hospital stay. I had moments of coming in and out of conscious awareness; and "moments" is exactly the correct word—nothing more than a glimpse, so short you can't really define it. One evening, upon my first brush of memory, I was being given meds by one of the nurses. As she handed me the medication I was led to question her whether it was my medicine. It looked different. Having no memory to that point, I have after wondered how I knew that. She looked, and all of a sudden said, "Oh Mrs. Rogers, I am sorry" and left the room. She came back with different medication. I still wasn't with it enough to let it bother me a great deal at the time, but when I think about the timing of regaining my awareness enough to ward off what could have been a major error, I am overwhelmed.

I don't remember going back to sleep, but I do remember when I woke up, I felt rather perplexed with my surroundings and all that had happened. I felt estranged. At that moment, I found myself opening the drawer of the dresser next to my bed and reaching for the Bible, almost as if I knew it was there. I simply opened it to Psalms; it was automatic. I read one verse and it said to me, "Sloan, you are going to be fine." Peace settled in, and I went on to recuperate. To this day, I cannot find the verse that I read, but the message I needed at that moment was given to me.

I was very anxious about taking a long drive back to Pennsylvania upon getting out of the hospital. I hadn't yet felt a total grasp of all that had transpired.

Carole being in Pennsylvania at that time meant a lot to me as she certainly supported me in the healing process which was not only quite painful, but included a number of visual disturbances.

Aside from work, I was very active in my church and Blue Bell Rotary (a charter member). I gave up the latter after recuperating.

In 1987, I married my husband of twenty years who died in 2007 after a lengthy six-year stretch of comorbidity.

During my deceased husband's last two years, he suggested that we give up the home we were living in to scale down, knowing that as things were going, I would probably be widowed, and needing to take care of myself. He suggested that I look for a place in the area where Carole and my mother were sharing a home.

The first day I went out looking, I found a home across the street and about five houses up from where Carole and my mother lived. Long story shortened, we purchased our last home together. It was the closest Carole and I had lived together in many years. It can be reassuring to have family close by when challenges mount.

Our lives became slightly more intertwined. At one juncture, after a major surgery, my husband was in a hospital, rehab, and nursing home for over six months in total. I would visit him each day after work, driving an hour each way. When he was at Thomas Jefferson Hospital, Carole would come in the evenings and ride home with me, knowing how tired I was from working, traveling, and being caregiver and advocate for my ill husband. She had observed my tiredness. Sometimes when I would be driving the last mile to home, I would almost seem to be in a state of limbo, fighting not to go to sleep. Her help was so appreciated.

After my husband passed away, I was able to help Carole with needs my mom had in the aging process as she moved from her home to assisted living to skilled care. My working in an exceptional retirement company with a large number of communities, we were able to find the best care for my mother.

Between Carole and me, we were there almost every day to visited our mother almost every day. Our oldest children who lived in the area, Susan and Stephen, and his wife Kim, were a blessing, too, in the support they rendered. My mother loved her grandchildren.

You might muse to know that as I am writing, I feel slightly challenged whether to refer to mother as, "my mother" or "our mother." Either seems to work.

I recall instances of either Carole or me referring to "my" mother and the other one would say, "She's my mother, too."

In later years, Carole had developed a special relationship with my mother. They had lived together for a number of years before her passing away. Actually, I guess each of my mother's daughters had their own unique relationship. Dawn came as often as she could from the Maryland shore. That was a time for us all to get together, though Carole and I would be sure to give Dawn some alone time with mom.

Carole had an outgoing way of relating to the people in the skilled care community that I am sure added to the quality of my mom's care. Though more reserved, I could also make things happen, but it would be with a different style—more subtle. In the initial period of my mother needing extra care, I was somewhat drained from caring for late husband for the previous six years.

There would be times when one of us would ask the other to take care of a particular issue, i.e., "Will you please make this call" with whatever the reason might be. Normally it didn't take too many back and forth's to come to an agreement. We all wanted the best care that could be provided for mother.

I'm thinking about how many adventures or fun things Carole and I did together while we were both living in Blue Bell. Our lives kind of revolved around work, family gatherings, birthday dinner parties, an occasional movie, shopping together, and attending an event or two.

There was a trip where Carole and I took mother to Long Branch in New Jersey the year before she went into assisted living. It was truly a joint venture. By that point, mother was in a wheelchair as opposed to walking distances, which made the trip a little tedious, but fun.

Our children also surprised us with a most wonderful 60th birthday party. The theme was being on a cruise liner and I must say that, short of the actual water, we had quite an event.

While we were experiencing the earlier Pennsylvania years, we were each rather independent—Checking in from time to time, pooling our energies from time to time, and being there for each other when the need dictated.

My work experience had gotten exasperating for me. I found it difficult to move from my position as an Administrative Assistant to the Vice President of Sales and Marketing to a Receptionist position while continuing with some of the work I had been doing. The company had to make some major changes due to the economy, and while I was grateful, they had found a way to keep me employed, my past seven years were screaming at me to be free and not confined behind a desk.

Good fortune brought a special partner into my life and I was able to retire and move to DC.

Most importantly, within this relationship, I am cared about, respected, understood, and encouraged to be the best I can be. Raina and I are miles apart again, these are not insurmountable miles should the need or desire dictate.

## by: Carole

I am always amazed by how life unfolds perfectly or not so seemingly perfect. Some twenty years ago, when I was living in Connecticut, I got a call from Elaine to come to Blue Bell, Pennsylvania, for an interview with the affiliate company she was working for. Not many years before this call, which would change my life, I had visited her and thought to myself, *There is absolutely no way I would ever live here in this "landlocked country."* I did not like the tree-studded roads that hid the beautiful sky, and I would dearly miss being by the water, a love of my life.

Today, I feel so grateful to Elaine for having mentioned me to Jack Toebe, my boss, when he asked her if she knew anyone like herself. I will never forget coming down for the interview. It was wonderful, and everything went beautifully. I asked the Lord for guidance to make the right decision, because I was leaving my family behind in Connecticut where I was living and had grown up.

During the three-hour interview, I got a nudge from the universe helping me to make my decision. There on Jack's wall was a group of pictures that his lovely wife, Patty, had put together for him in his office. Right there in the middle was a picture of

Jack with the words, "Dickie Bird." I had all the confirmation I needed. Now that is exactly what my grandmother used to call my father when he was a little boy. How many "Dickie Birds" do you know? I would expect that your answer is none. That is my point. And on top of this, when I looked at Jack from a certain angle, I could see an uncanny resemblance to my father. After the interview, I ran to my sister who was in the next office and said, "Do you see what I see?" and she confirmed she did. Aren't the messages that life gives incredible? Oh, yes, if we are open to receive them. Jack made me an offer and I accepted the position.

When I arrived in Blue Bell for my new job, I was without money, except for a gift of one thousand dollars given to me by a dear friend who believed in me and in my move to Philadelphia, and a car full of my worldly possessions.

I moved into a nice little apartment with only a bed and an occasional chair that Elaine had given me. I have always felt a strong sense of responsibility and I wanted to do this on my own. But I allowed myself to graciously accept the bare necessities from her. And, further I didn't want to be a burden to anyone and reminded myself adamantly moment by moment, "I can do this". Week in and week out, I came home and made myself a picnic for dinner on the middle of the dining room floor on a comforter. I could have called it a quilt but it was my warmth so to speak, so comforter felt appropriate.

For several weeks, I had been trying to get credit but nothing seemed to be working. Because of being new in the area and not having stability in the job yet, I was constantly being turned down. This particular night I pulled my comforter over to the living room wall, rested my body against the wall, and started crying, and the tears just flowed. I said to God, whom I talked to daily, "I can't do this anymore I need some furniture." My sister called in the middle of my tears and said it will be all right and something would work out. She had a way of doing that, and I did with her. The next morning when I arrived at work and sat down at my desk, my phone was ringing. It was a company I hadn't heard of offering me a loan. I jumped up *so* excitedly and ran to tell Elaine about it. She was in as much disbelief as I was. I borrowed the money, modestly furnished my apartment, and went on with my life. If I didn't fully understood the message, "Let go and let God," Then I do now. God was indeed my source.

For some time I repeatedly asked myself, "What are you doing here? What was I thinking to leave my family back in Connecticut?"

One day there was a redeeming moment that I can profoundly remember. I was coming home from work and as I came over the hill on a road that I traveled every day, I looked ahead with new eyes and saw the most incredible sunset. I instantly picked up my cell phone and called everyone I could think of to see if they saw this exquisite sunset, too. Looking back now, the receivers of my calls must have thought I was a little crazy to be as excited as I was. Then, they had no idea of how I longed to be back again in the open spaces by the water.

Shortly after, when I was on my way to work, I ran into the store to get something. I was feeling lonely and missing my family left behind in Connecticut. I wondered if this feeling would ever go away. As I came out, I looked across the parking lot, and high in the sky was this little bird flying all alone. I said, to myself, "Hi, little bird, I know how you feel way up there all by yourself," and as I was looking up across the sky, a splash of water hit my eye. From whence it cometh, I have no idea, but I do know it was to catch my attention. And the words came to me. "But you are never alone; I am always with you." At that very instant, great peace flowed through my body, traveling from my head to my toes. I have never felt alone since that moment. I drove on to work nestled in the comfort that this was going to be my home and all was good.

In my peace, I was able to realize fully that for the third time since Elaine and I were in our early twenties, we were going to be living in the same area. How amazing! The two previous times were many years before, when for a very short period, I lived in Maryland and Pennsylvania with her. But I knew this time was going to be different. I was in for the long haul.

Somewhere along the way after settling in, I began to feel there were many reasons why I needed to be here that would be revealed. I felt these feelings from time to time. My mother was quite intuitive, and I believe I have some of that deeper insight, too.

The last twenty years of my life spent in Blue Bell have been bittersweet. It has been a journey that I have come to believe was meant to be as I indicated. When I look at how these years have unfolded, I understand these earlier feelings more clearly. For how much longer, I do not know. I am not certain how much longer I will live here. for there is a part of me that still longs to live by the water before I transition from this life experience.

There was an event when Elaine, her husband, and I were in Connecticut for a weekend. When Elaine arrived, she was in serious distress. Her husband ran into the house to call 911. As he did, I ran out to the car to see what I could do for her. She was in an obviously critical way, and she was not communicating on a cognitive level. I tried to make sense of what was going on, but I knew she needed to be in the hospital urgently. Within minutes, the ambulance arrived and she was whisked away. We followed her to the hospital to find out that she had had major bleeding in the brain. Now statistics say that one-third do not make it from the start, one-third last about 2 weeks, and one-third have post-trauma difficulties. Then there is that miracle that occurs once in a blue moon. Elaine was one of the miracles. Thank you, God.

The hours were long in awaiting her fate, but I knew I had to go into prayer, and the only gift I could give to her at this time was seeing her whole and perfect. I could not let myself fall into the "human" aspect of this event. I would give her love and only positive energy. That was my gift. I would not see the possibility of any of the statistics. I held on to knowing that she was going to be better than ever. It was my undying prayer—more like a mantra.

I came to visit Elaine from Blue Bell to Connecticut every day after work while she was in the ICU. I had to work, because my boss was in Florida, and I was needed in the office. It was difficult to commute two and a half hours each way on a daily basis. There were times I wondered if I would make it, but I would pull over along the side of the road, sleep a little, and continue. If one never believed in God's grace, they would have come to know it as I did. It was undeniable. Alone, I could not have survived those trips. When Elaine arrived home a week or so later, she was in a great deal of discomfort and feeling anxious about what she had just experienced. I became like an appendage to her. For three months, I was over to her home every lunchtime and after work, trying to bring peace and comfort to her healing journey. As Mother would say, "You go, girl." I am so grateful to say that she had a complete healing. *There was no doubt I needed to be here.*

A relatively new friend, whom I didn't know well, invited me to celebrate his birthday. I could not decide what to take him for a gift. I had no real idea, but I decided to pray on it, and as I did, what came to me was a book that I loved. It was called *Power Through Constructive Thinking* by Emmett Fox. I loved this little book and found much peace in its words along the way. There were many times I had given it as a present, so this was feeling better than good to me for reasons that I could not explain. It was the kind of book you would give to someone you knew really well. Following my inner dictate, I presented this friend with Emmett Fox's book. Maybe four months later, my quasi friend came to me and asked if we could talk. He told me that, from time to time, he had thought about taking his life, but after he read the book, he found such purpose for being here that those thoughts seemed to subside tremendously and he no longer had that feeling. I can still hear his words when he said, "You saved my life." Again, it was clear, *there was no doubt I needed to be here.*

Not many years later, Elaine's husband became ill and it was a long journey of about six years filled with medical issues and several major surgeries. I knew I needed to be by her side as much as I could. And, I wanted to be. We traveled to Hopkins for one major surgery and to Center City, Philadelphia, for the others. For weeks at a time, Elaine would work and go straight to the hospital. I do not believe she ever missed a day. One time as I was driving behind her, I became aware that she was very groggy at the wheel and fortunately awoke before having an accident. I was so concerned for her that, every day after work, a friend of mine and I would drive to the city to make certain she got home safely. She was in autopilot; that was for sure. I remember times helping them in the middle of the night or whenever the need arose. Yes, once again, I knew *there was no doubt I needed to be here.*

As I was nearing my third year in Pennsylvania, I had gone to the shore, which was only an hour and a half away, to visit my daughters. My mother, who had been visiting my older sister, met us a day later. She took sick shortly after arriving at the shore, and I rode by her side in the ambulance, back to Blue Bell where I lived, because she needed treatment in a hospital, and that was the only way I could help her. She never ended up leaving Blue Bell. She lived seventeen years here with me. Within about five years, I became her caregiver. It was about four years before she died. I could not take care of mother and work my full-time job any longer. I would be up most of the night, tending to her needs. She ended up going into an assisted care community. It was the only way to provide the care she needed. It hurt us all. Elaine and I did promise to visit her every day the first three months to see how it would work. She believed one should live and die in their home. Yes, that would be beautiful if it were possible. However, we did not have the financial luxury to make that happen. After the three months went by, she said she would be okay, and I visited her no less than three or four times a week, until the day she died. Yes, *there was no doubt I needed to be here.*

My first book was written in Blue Bell. Aaron Graves a talented musician, composer audio book. *I needed to be here.*

My life did not allow for too much outside of work or helping where I saw the need. My life was full, and I was longing for a relationship. I did have a companion whom I lived with for five years. He was a tremendous help with my mother and my sister's husband, but he, too, became sick. He actually passed away three days before Mother. He had moved out two years prior to work on a project he wanted to complete and could not do from here. While we were still close, we did not see much of each other except when my daughter and I would journey to the hospital to see him where he was for a year and a half before his death.

In the midst of these life situations, my youngest daughter and two of my grandchildren blessed me with their presence in Blue Bell. Cher was making some life changes, and I was thrilled to have her, happy to help her get settled in any way I could. It was exciting to have some of my grands close by. I missed my girls and my grands so much when I came here. They lived in Connecticut near me. Little did I know that my oldest daughter, Susan, would grace my life with her presence in Blue Bell. The only one missing was my middle daughter, Dawn. That would have been perfect.

In reflection, I realize that I spent a good two-thirds of my life in a caregiver's roll in one way or another while working full-time. Daddy had been sick for twelve years prior to my coming to Philly, and we were told that he would not make morning seven times. Yes, seven times my mother and I called my sisters to Connecticut to find that he pulled through yet another time. He died two days after Elaine and I had come together to celebrate our fortieth birthday.

I would like to take a moment to talk about my position with the Klenzoid Equipment Company. This is no ordinary company. I was excited, because the company matched my business ethics. This was essential to me. It is an integral company with high business standards, always striving to put the customer first. When my boss, Jack, retired, his son, John, became the president of the company. This was a beautiful thing, too. The spirit of the company is to offer each employee the freedom to create an office to reflect one's authentic self. This was important to me also. Often I would tell John this is my home away from home. This was the caveat. Just being in the office and with my customers was a respite from the demands of life that would be waiting for me when I returned home in the evening. In spite of the needs that were going on in my life, I gratefully continued to excel in my job.

As the years melted one into the other, I began to feel a stirring that I needed to consider my life's desires.

Two months after Mother and my friend, Rick, passed away, Elaine made a decision to move to Washington, DC, to fulfill her life in a grander way. She was the impetus that brought me here, and now she was leaving, too. There were so many separations for me in such a short period; I wondered how to process this loss. I guess my body did, too. One evening out of the blue, as I went to climb the seventeen steps that lead to my upper level, I could not make it. My leg would not hold my weight. I knew something was very wrong. Long story short, I found an amazing doctor who is so much more than a chiropractor. He is a healer in every sense of the word. His words resounded to me when he said, "*You are the ultimate healer. I am here to assist in your journey.*" Yes, he was on my team, and I was grateful. Only nights before, I was to be led to him, I lay in my bed and consciously made the decision

I would overcome this. There was a brief moment I thought my body was shutting down and I was not going to make it. A year later, I am filled with a strong and gradual but constant healing journey that affords me glimmers of wholeness I don't believe I have ever known. Thank you gratefully, Dr. Paul Mychaluk. Yet, another time *there is no doubt that I needed to be here.*

I do want you to know that laced in these years were wonderful times and celebrations. We are a party family and recognize those occasions to celebrate with each other, and we surely do that—birthdays, weddings, graduations. These are times when distance does not stand in the way. We come together in love and tribute to the guest of honor.

I believe I could actually write a whole book on my twenty years here. I would like to conclude by saying that living in Blue Bell has brought me on a closer walk with God (interestingly the name of my first book). It brought me: the opportunity to live near my sister, Elaine, until she moved to another state (as serendipity would have it), my other sister, Dawn, close by, the opportunity to take care of my mother in her last years, the chance to achieve pieces of my dream, cherished friendships that I dearly treasure—once in a lifetime kind of friendships, the writing of this book, *Rocking to Different Drummers*, and a greater insight for my sense of loss that I have mentioned to you.

Working on our book has heightened, for me, the truths of our upbringing, and it has awakened a deeper understanding of my relationship with my sister.

As I recalled walking along in nature early on and thinking how alone I felt even though I dearly loved my sisters, there was this sense of missing something in my life, something I could not explain. However, this feeling was always buffered along the way because I had my twin sister, Elaine, and my sister, Dawn, close by. I have two sister-friends. That is when life makes you sisters and love makes you friends. On rare occasions, I would refer to Dawn as Mom; that is how special she is.

Then it came to me, as the history of our lives has been replayed, whether it was the strong desire of our mother to raise us with a decided sense for individuality to cover up her disappoint in losing her triplet. As I embrace this possibility, I wonder if I was missing what my mother had lost. I don't know this, but perhaps calling us "twins" may have served to be a hurtful and constant reminder. Or maybe it was a little of both. Either way creating our independence was a blessing that she gave us. That being said, I am deeply sorry for her loss and mine.

When I look at and review our stance for individuality, I am struck by the stunning likeness in the three tests we did for you, revealing our personalities. I would not have expected this likeness to be so similar.

What it says to me is that, in the choices to be individually unique, coupled with the role that the environment played in our lives, one thing stands strong and clear: there is a likeness that exists simply by being a twin.

I reflect back on my words when first arriving in Blue Bell and affectionately say I am blessed for having spent the last twenty years in this "*land locked country.*"

# How You See Me and Me

## ABOUT THE FLOWERS

As you may imagine to determine the perfect one word to describe a person takes a great deal of thought. It is quite difficult to find one word that aptly says it all, however these five people from different areas of our life have graciously given time and consideration to their concepts as to how they view each of us.

Dr. Lawrence Borow is a highly esteemed OB-GYN in Bala Cynwyd, PA. We have had the good fortune of being in his remarkable care of over 30 years.

Rev. Sheila Pierce is the founding minister of Circle of Peace in Elkins Park, PA. She has been a dear friend of Carole's and the family sharing in special life experiences for over 16 years.

John M. Toebe is the President of Klenzoid Equipment Company in Blue Bell, PA and has worked with Carole and been a friend of both Carole and Elaine for over 20 years. Elaine worked with John as well for a short time when employed by their affiliate company.

Lucy Arnold is a close family friend who we have shared many special life experiences with for over 14 years. Lucy and Carole worked together at Klenzoid Equipment Company for several years.

Dawn Ganss is our sister – One could say she had the best seat in the house.

# HOW I AM SEEN

John Toebe says: Driven

Rev. Sheila Pierce says: Tenacious

Dr. Borow says: Mystical

Lucy says: Enduring

Dawn says: Genuine & Compassionate

*Elaine*

# Personality Inventories

What do they say about us?

We will not be giving all the specifics of each test, but enough information to share the comparison in our results.

As independent and different as we see ourselves, the results prove to be rather interesting. Each test was taken in an informal setting, each of us in our respective homes and only comparing the results.

---
❧
---

## MYERS BRIGGS TYPE INDICATOR®

Myers Briggs Type Indicator® appeared on the scene in the mid-1900s. Millions of people have taken this inventory in which there are no right or wrong answers. It is defined by sixteen personality types. There are eight categories and each person taking the test will be ascribed four categories to determine their personality type.

The categories are:

| | | |
|---|---|---|
| (E) Extroverted | OR | (I) Introverted |
| (S) Sensing | OR | (N) Intuitive |
| (T) Thinking | OR | (F) Feeling |
| (J) Judging | OR | (P) Perceiving |

The below percentages reflect the degree we are within a particular characteristic.

Note, we each have the same personality type with slightly varying percentages

|   |            | **Elaine** | **Carole** |
|---|------------|--------|--------|
| I | Introverted | 22%    | 11%    |
| N | Intuitive   | 50%    | 25%    |
| F | Feeling     | 50%    | 50%    |
| J | Judging     | 11%    | 22%    |

The above shows that Elaine at 22 percent is 11 percent more introverted than Carole whose test reflected 11 percent. Also, minus that 11 percent for Carole and 22 percent for Elaine they would be moving into the extroversion range.

Elaine first took this inventory when in her thirties and came out with the same result again.

Both Elaine and Carole are INFJs, which represent 1 to 3 percent of the population

A glance at those characteristics:

| I | Introverted | Thinks and reflects before acting. |
|---|-------------|-------------------------------------|
|   |             | Uses "private time" to recharge energy. |
|   |             | Motivated internally; when mind is active can "close" out outside world. |
|   |             | One-on-one relationships and conversation most preferred. |

| N | Intuition | Mentally attends to future possibilities. |
|---|---|---|
| | | Imaginative and creative, seeing new possibilities instinctual. |
| | | Recall emphasis is on contexts, patterns and connections. |
| | | Theoretical understanding provides best improvisations. |
| | | Comfortable with guessing meanings when ambiguous and unclear data is provided. |
| F | Feeling | Innately looks to personal feelings and implication for others when making decisions. |
| | | Naturally sensitive to the reaction and needs of others. |
| | | Naturally looks for popular opinions and consensus. |
| | | Views conflict as very unsettling. |
| J | Judging | Before taking action, plans details in advance. |
| | | Focuses on completing meaningful segments of a task before moving forward. |
| | | By keeping ahead of deadlines avoids stress and does best work. |
| | | Manages life naturally, using target, dates and routines. |

## HOWARD GARDNER INTELLIGENCE TEST

Howard Gardner, in 1983, outlined his theory regarding kinds of intelligence. He defined eight different kinds of "intelligences." These represent talents, personality traits, and abilities.

What his testing suggests is that people have different intelligences as opposed to an intellectual capacity.

Those eight intelligences are:

Linguistic/Verbal
Logical/Mathematical
Musical
Spatial/Visual
Bodily/Kinesthetic
Intrapersonal
Interpersonal
Naturalist
Existential (This factor was added later on)

The findings are evaluated on a scale where results are either above or below a mid-line, each side reflecting a count of 0 to 12 above or -0 to -12 below. Most people will have at least two intelligent factors above the line, which reflect their greater abilities.

Elaine and Carole had three areas above the line:

|  | **Elaine** | **Carole** |
|---|---|---|
| Intrapersonal | 8 | 10 |
| Visual/Spatial | 8 | 8 |
| Linguistic Verbal | 4 | 2 |

| Intrapersonal | Good at evaluating/analyzing strengths and weaknesses |
| | Has pleasure in analyzing ideas and theories |
| | Self-awareness is exceptional |
| | Basis for motivation and feelings is clearly understood |
| Visual/ Spatial | Reading and writing are enjoyed |
| | Putting puzzles together comes easy |
| | Painting, drawing and visual arts are enjoyed |
| | Patterns are easily recognized |
| Linguistic Verbal | Written and spoken information well remembered |
| | Reading and writing enjoyable |
| | Good debating and persuasive skills |
| | Explains things well |
| | Uses humor when writing or telling stories |

## THE BIG FIVE AND DIMENSIONAL TEST FOR IDENTICAL TWINS

*Twins: A research interactive personality test*

We thought it would be fun to do this test that has been designed for depicting the similarities and the differences in the personalities of twins to share with you, our readers.

The test is designed with two main parts:
The "Big Five"

# The Dimensional Assessment in Personalities

*Comparison results between Elaine and Carole*

As to the overall, we fell into a percentile shy of 97 percent regarding our similarities. What that meant is that only three to four out of one hundred people are more similar.

| | | |
|---|---|---|
| Overall Low Similarity | xxxxxxxxxxxxxxxxxxxxxxxxxxxxxOxx | Overall High Similarity |
| Low Big Five Similarity | xxxxxxxxxxxxxxxxxxxxxxxxxxxxxOx | Very Similar for Big Five |
| Low Dimensional Assessment | xxxxxxxxxxxxxxxxxxxxxxxxOxxxxxx | High Dimensional Assessment |

*"Big Five" Results Between Elaine and Carole*

This is often referred to as the OCEAN model of personality and by many considered the best survey to describe a personality.

Our similarity percentile is 99.35.

Carole's Results

| | | |
|---|---|---|
| Closed Minded | xxxxxxxxxxxxxxxxxOxxxxxxx | Open to New Experiences |
| Disorganized | xxxxxxxxxxxxxxxxxxxxxxOxx | Conscientious |
| Introverted | xxxxxxxxxxxxxxxxxOxxxxxxx | Extroverted |
| Disagreeable | xxxxxxxxxxxxxxxxxxxxOxx | Agreeable |
| Calm/Relaxed | xxxOxxxxxxxxxxxxxxxxxxxxx | Nervous/ High Strung |

Elaine's Results

| | | |
|---|---|---|
| Closed Minded | xxxxxxxxxOxxxxxxxxxxxxx | Open to New Experiences |
| Disorganized | xxxxxxxxxxxxxxxxxxxxOxx | Conscientious |
| Introverted | xxxxxxxOxxxxxxxxxxxxxxxx | Extroverted |

| Disagreeable | xxxxxxxxxxxxxxxxxxxxxxxxOxx | Agreeable |
| Calm/Relaxed | xxOxxxxxxxxxxxxxxxxxxxxxxxx | Nervous/High Strung |

## Summary of "Big Five"

Carole is more open to new experiences; Elaine usually does not seek out new experiences.

Both Carole and Elaine are well organized and can be relied upon.

Carole is more social, enjoying the company of others; Elaine tends to shy away from social situations.

Both Carole and Elaine are supportive, good natured and courteous.

Both Carole and Elaine are likely to remain calm, even in tense situations.

*Dimensional Assessment in Personality Between Elaine & Carole*

Our similarity percentile is 71.7.

This survey describes preferences and behaviors relating to: feelings, personal characteristics, relationships with others and thinking skills.

## Carole's Results

| Affect Stability | xxxxxxxxxxxxOxxxxxxxxxxxxxx | High Affect |
| Settled Sense of Self | xOxxxxxxxxxxxxxxxxxxxxxxxxx | Changing Sense of Self |
| Interpersonally Highly Independent | xxxxxxxOxxxxxxxxxxxxxxxxxxx | Interpersonally Highly Involved |
| Highly Factual | xxxOxxxxxxxxxxxxxxxxxxxxxxx | Highly Imaginative |

## Elaine's Results

| | | |
|---|---|---|
| Affect Stability | xxxxxxxxOxxxxxxxxxxxxxxxxxxxx | High Affect |
| Settled Sense of Self | xxxxxOxxxxxxxxxxxxxxxxxxxxxxx | Changing Sense of Self |
| Interpersonally Highly Independent | xxxxxxxxxxOxxxxxxxxxxxxxxxxx | Interpersonally Highly Involved |
| Highly Factual | xOxxxxxxxxxxxxxxxxxxxxxxxxxxx | Highly Imaginative |

*Summary of Dimensional Assessment*

Carole expresses emotion with occasional mood changes; Elaine expresses emotions consistently with moods that are stable and predictable.

Both Carole and Elaine have a true sense of self, rarely showing boredom.

Both Carole and Elaine cope well with separation from those they are close to, rarely fearing rejection.

Both Carole and Elaine rarely experience things they feel are strange.

We both feel that neither similarity nor difference alone predicts the quality of a relationship.

# Epilogue

---

## FINAL THOUGHTS
*by Elaine/Sloan*

In the process of writing *Rocking to Different Drummers*, Carole and I have been focusing on our twin relationship in a way that we never have in the past.

The focus clearly started out with the intent of looking at our differences and keeping with the philosophy of supporting individualism that was ever present during our formative years.

What has surprised me the most was to discover that, while our style and interpretations were quite different, we tended to remember the same instances within each segment of our writing. There were some difficult moments in the recollecting and understanding of our different perceptions. Our struggles were short lived. What I came to realize was that Carole and I were so much on our own path growing up that we had very, very few confrontations. However, we were never so diverted on those paths that we were not there for each other when a need arose. Even still, one might ask if we were protesting too much. Did we lose a unique camaraderie in the process?

Given an opportunity to change anything, I would still strive for autonomy. The ability to fully love and reach out is rooted in one's autonomy.

Most remarkable, to us, was the likeness with which we tested on the personality, intelligence, and dimensional inventories.

All and all, for Carole and me, nothing has changed. Life continues as it was before we gave such focus on our kinship.

## FINAL THOUGHTS
### by Carole/Raina

The writing of this book with my sister has interestingly revealed to me that I do not see anything startlingly different in our life today as opposed to how it has been over the years. I found it surprising to see how we viewed the same events so differently and yet in discussing them we both feel strongly about our own views.

However, even more surprising to me were the things I did not remember until Elaine's memories revealed them. This makes me wonder if in the earlier days of my life the loneliness I couldn't articulate even to myself, let alone to another, caused the impression of events in my earlier life to be elusive. In spite of this elusiveness are the feelings that I was never really understood by my family. I have always been told that I have a different way of expressing myself, and I wondered if writing this book with Elaine would bring a greater understanding to them. I want my two beautiful sisters to know that part of me. I wonder if they do now.

As I look at this broad-brush of my life, it became more profound to me that I have always been responsible even in my weakest moments. Just as profound was how I had been there for others' needs before some of my own. Gratefully, I made the decision to fulfill my desires. Fortunately, it is never too late. I have learned the more fully we can express our true nature, the more yet we have to give.

There were sad moments in some of our differences, but great joy to share in the outcome. One thing I came to see more clearly is that each step in our life brings us closer to a greater awareness whether it be through joy or pain. How beautiful to never lose sight that joy is our birthright. Amen.

# Citations

Burack, Marsha. *Reiki Healing Yourself and Others*. Lo Ro Production, 1995

Dispenza, Dr. Joe. *Breaking the Habit of Being Yourself*. Hay House, 2013.

National Institute of Environmental Health Sciences, "Billy Boy." http://kids.niehs.nih.gov/games/songs/childrens/billyboymid.htm.

"Phenomena." Webster's New World Dictionary and Thesaurus, Second Edition, pg 477. 2002.

"Phenotypically Concordant and Discordant Monozygotic Twins Display Different DNA Copy-Number-Variation Profiles." Carl E.G. Bruder, Arkadiusz Piotrowski, et al. *The American Journal of Human Genetics*—3 March 2008 (Vol. 82, Issue 3, pp. 763-771)

Wordsworth, William. Poets.org, "The Daffodils." Accessed August 23, 2013. http://www.poets.org/viewmedia.php/prmMID/15925.

Let life be a joyous journey
Carole and Elaine

Here's to you!
Raina and Sloan